GOD'S TRANSFORMING WORD

How to Study Your Bible

THOMAS D. LEA

Learning Exercises by Bill Latham
Leader Guide by Don Atkinson

LIfeWay Press
Nashville, Tennessee

ISBN 0-6330-2948-3

This book is the text for course CG-0102 in the subject area Bible Studies
in the Christian Growth Study Plan.

Dewey Decimal Classification Number: 248.4
Subject Headings: CHRISTIAN LIFE \ SALVATION

Unless stated otherwise, the Scripture quotations in this book are from
the *New American Standard Bible.* Copyright © The Lockman Foundation,
1960, 1962, 1963, 1968, 1971, 1972, 1973, 1975, 1977. Used by permission.

Order additional copies of this book by writing to LifeWay Church Resources
Customer Service, MSN 113; 127 Ninth Avenue, North; Nashville, TN 37234;
by calling (800) 458-2772; by faxing (615) 251-5933; by ordering online at
www.lifeway.com; by emailing *customerservice@lifeway.com;*
or by visiting a LifeWay Christian Store.

For information about adult discipleship and family resources,
training, and events, visit our Web site at *www.lifeway.com/discipleplus.*

Printed in the United States of America

LifeWay Press
127 Ninth Avenue, North
Nashville, Tennessee 37234-0151

*As God works through us, we will help people and churches
know Jesus Christ and seek His kingdom by providing biblical solutions
that spiritually transform individuals and cultures.*

THOMAS D. LEA

To the memory of Thomas D. Lea, whose commitment to Bible study
and whose faithful service as a seminary professor and writer
instilled in thousands of believers a love for God's Word and
a desire to discover its transforming truths.

The Lord's lovingkindnesses indeed never cease,
For His compassions never fail.
They are new every morning;
Great is Thy faithfulness.
Lamentations 3:22-23

❧ The Authors ☙

Thomas D. Lea wrote the content for *God's Transforming Word: How to Study Your Bible*. Prior to his death in 1999, Lea was the dean of Southwestern Baptist Theological Seminary's School of Theology and served as a professor of New Testament for 20 years. Before joining the seminary faculty, Lea pastored churches in Alabama, Virginia, and Texas.

A native of Houston, Mississippi, Lea was a graduate of Mississippi State University and held master of divinity and doctor of theology degrees from Southwestern Baptist Theological Seminary. Lea was frequently a conference leader and teacher at state and national conference centers and a writer for journals and denominational publications. In addition to this course, he wrote or cowrote *Step by Step Through the New Testament* (LifeWay Press), *MasterDesign: Your Calling as a Christian* (LifeWay Press), and *The New Testament—Its Background and Message* (Broadman & Holman Publishers).

In a 1992 interview Lea was quoted as saying, "My years in seminary taught me how to study the Bible, gave me the desire to study the Bible and to help other people learn about it as well." As a participant in *God's Transforming Word*, you are the privileged recipient not only of Lea's great wealth of knowledge but also of his lifelong passion for teaching believers how to study and live God's Word.

Bill Latham wrote the practical learning exercises for this course. Latham received a bachelor of arts degree from Mississippi College and a bachelor of divinity degree from New Orleans Baptist Theological Seminary. His professional ministry includes 7 years as a minister of education; 10 years as the director of adult work in the Training Union Department of the Mississippi Baptist Convention; and until his retirement in 1995, more than 19 years as an editor of Discipleship Training materials at LifeWay Christian Resources. Through the years of his professional ministry and in retirement, Latham has been a contributing writer to a variety of curriculum and leisure-reading materials.

Don Atkinson wrote the leader guide. Atkinson is an editor of adult discipleship resources at LifeWay Christian Resources. Prior to coming to LifeWay, he served as the pastor of several churches in his home state of Alabama, as well as in Georgia and Kentucky. In addition to his editorial career, Atkinson is the pastor of Walker Memorial Baptist Church in Franklin, Tennessee. Atkinson received a bachelor of arts degree from Athens College, bachelor of divinity and master of divinity degrees from Southern Baptist Theological Seminary, and a doctor of ministry degree from New Orleans Baptist Theological Seminary.

CONTENTS

❧ INTRODUCTION ❧

The law of the Lord is perfect,
restoring the soul;
The testimony of the Lord is
sure, making wise the simple.
The precepts of the Lord are
right, rejoicing the heart;
The commandment of the Lord
is pure, enlightening the eyes.
Psalm 19:7-8

What You Will Learn
- Guidelines for interpreting the Bible
- Principles for applying the Bible
- Ways to do Bible study
- How to apply Bible study
- Keys to understanding the Bible

In these verses the psalmist expressed the importance of Scripture in your Christian journey. God can use Scripture to revive you, give you wisdom, bring you joy, and open your eyes spiritually. God's Word will transform your life.

God's Transforming Word: How to Study Your Bible will guide you to develop skills for reading, understanding, and applying God's Word. You will approach the Bible with several different methods of study. Using these methods can provide a many-sided view of the Bible's contents. You will learn how to approach an entire book of the Bible or a brief passage. You will learn how to study a Bible character or a character trait. You will learn how to investigate the history, geography, and culture depicted in the Bible. You will also learn how to understand the theology of a passage and how to apply a passage to your life.

What You Will Learn

This study provides nine weeks of daily lessons that lead you through the following Bible-study topics.

Guidelines for Interpreting the Bible

In week 1 you will learn the following guidelines for accurately interpreting what the Bible says.
- Understand the writer's meaning.
- Observe the context.
- Accept the limits of revelation.
- Identify the type of writing.
- Use the Bible to interpret itself.

These lessons will help you study the Bible with more accuracy and insight.

Principles for Applying the Bible

In week 2 you will learn principles for applying the message of the Bible to your life.
- Apply the Bible according to its real meaning.
- Use the Bible as a book of principles.

- Use the promises properly.
- Use as cross-cultural understanding.
- Use the Bible wisely.

Ways to Do Bible Study
The lessons for weeks 3–5 will teach you how to do three types of Bible study.

- Synthetic Bible study is a method you will use to approach a complete book of the Bible. You will learn how to overview what the book is teaching and how to outline the book.
- Analytical Bible study allows you to study a brief passage of Scripture, seeking to understand its content and apply it to your life.
- Background Bible study explores the history, geography, and culture of the Bible. Learning background facts can make the Bible come to life and can help you understand portions that might otherwise be puzzling.

How to Apply Bible Study
The Bible has a message you can apply to your relationship with God, to your own life, to your relationships with others, and to the church. Weeks 6 and 7 will teach you how to apply the following types of Bible study to each area of your life.

- Biographical Bible study
- Character-trait Bible study
- Devotional Bible study

Keys to Understanding the Bible
Weeks 8 and 9 will present keys to understanding the Bible.

- You will learn how to understand the words and images that are used in the Bible.
- You will study the grammar of the Bible to improve your understanding of what God is saying.
- Your study of the topics of the Bible will give you an organized picture of what the Bible teaches on many subjects.
- You will learn to use the Bible to understand the doctrines taught in Scripture.

These studies will consist of different methods and principles that can improve your study habits in all your work with the Bible.

A Hunger for God's Word
If your life is to be transformed through Bible study, you must have a spiritual hunger for God's Word. Several qualities characterize someone who truly wants to know God's Word.

Characteristics of a Spiritually Hungry Bible Student
- Dependence on the Holy Spirit
- Eagerness to learn about God
- A teachable attitude
- Discipline

Dependence on the Holy Spirit
To hunger for and understand God's Word, you must first be a Christian. To an unbeliever, the teachings of Scripture often don't make sense, and its commands and promises may be puzzling and unrealistic. The primary

reason the Bible is clear only to Christians is that only they have the Holy Spirit. The Holy Spirit is the teacher of God's truths (see John 14:26). He makes God's commands and promises easier to understand and apply. John 16:13-15 identifies one specific task of the Holy Spirit as teaching you all the things God wants you to know. Imagine that! God Himself, in the person of the Holy Spirit, is beside you each time you open your Bible to study, and He will personally show you all the things He wants you to know about Himself.

First Corinthians 2:10-14 says some important things about the Holy Spirit's role as a teacher.

- God uses the Holy Spirit to be our teacher because the Holy Spirit knows the deep truths of God.
- The only way a person can learn the things of God is to learn them from the Spirit of God.
- We are able to receive God's truth because we have received the Spirit of God.
- God's truth is foolish to a person who is not a Christian because that person has not received the Holy Spirit.

What sort of information does the Holy Spirit teach? He won't provide biblical facts you can learn in a Bible dictionary. He won't provide a solution to disputed biblical facts. You won't learn the identity of the author of Hebrews by depending on the Holy Spirit.

The Holy Spirit will shape your attitudes and spiritual perception. He will develop within you a spiritually receptive outlook. He will heighten your intellect so that you can understand the doctrines of the Bible.

The Holy Spirit's role is to illuminate the Bible. He makes you wise about the Bible's contents. He doesn't take you beyond it. He is not in the business of giving revelation in addition to or contrary to the Bible. He builds on what is there and makes its meaning and application clear. The Holy Spirit is our ultimate and final teacher. No person can truthfully teach us anything that is contrary to the Holy Spirit or that the Holy Spirit is not willing to verify as true. In a very real sense all other persons, objects, printed materials, and opinions are merely resources the Holy Spirit uses to teach us about God.

How can you find the Holy Spirit's guidance in Bible study? Begin your Bible study with a prayer for guidance. Bible students who have been able to understand the Bible and teach others have always generously mixed prayer with their studies. Psalm 119 contains many such prayers. Read some of these prayers and use them as models of requests you can make to begin your study of the Bible.

When you begin studying the Bible, recognize that you have no reason to feel defeated. God has given you the best possible teacher in the Holy Spirit. God wants you to be positive and excited about Bible study. Your dependence on the Holy Spirit can bring this attitude into your Bible study.

Eagerness to Learn About God

Understanding the Bible also demands an eagerness to learn about God. How eager a Bible student are you?

We can identify at least three different types of Bible students. The first type studies the Bible but not because of a spiritual hunger for God's truths. These people study God's Word for secondary reasons like curiosity about religion and Bible facts or perhaps loyalty to a Bible-study group or to a teacher.

The second type of Bible student is the would-be student. He lets circumstances distract him from Bible study. These circumstances may include personal pleasure such as watching television or attending sports events. Job activity can make a person too tired to want to spend time in Bible study. Sickness or accidents can weaken a person so that he gets off the track of Bible study. This type of student may also let other people interfere with Bible study. For example, some Christians who began studying the Bible during a lunch break have quit when other workers labeled them as too religious. A college student may quit studying the Bible when a roommate complains about a desk light that is shining too late or too early.

The third type of Bible student allows his eagerness to learn and apply the Bible to overcome all obstacles. Psalm 1:2 pronounces God's blessings on a person whose "delight is in the law of the Lord" and who meditates on that law "day and night." These words describe a person who is eager to know and obey God. The psalmist pictures a person who conducts his life and business during the day by biblical principles. He measures his actions at the end of the day by God's standards in the Bible.

In Psalm 19:7-14 the psalmist shows a high regard for God's message by describing it with words like *perfect, sure, pure,* and *clean.* He is eager to learn the Bible because it warns him of pitfalls to avoid. It also promises him great rewards. He loves the Bible because it offers him inner cleansing. He is eager to study the Bible because it offers him victory over deceitful, enslaving sins.

Observe the devotion of the psalmist in Psalm 119:9-11. He wants cleansing, purity, and preservation from sin. He presents himself before God with obedience, commitment, and purity. He is eager to learn about God.

What needs do you have and what benefits do you hope to receive that make you want to be a better student of God's Word? Ask God to help you develop a genuine eagerness to study His Word and to help you deal with the distractions that would keep you from Bible study.

A Teachable Attitude

To be a student of God's Word, you must have a teachable attitude.

Psalm 119 says a lot about being willing to learn and respond to God's Word. In verse 24 the psalmist shows his delight in God's Word. It performs an important role of leadership in his life. The psalmist knows that he needs to understand what God has said. Verse 34 is a prayer for this understanding. The words of verse 105 again express the role of God's Word in giving leadership. Verse 108 expresses an openness, obedience, and willingness to learn. The last verse of the psalm expresses human weakness. The psalmist still recognizes that the Lord's commandments are a solution to his problems. Throughout this psalm the writer shows a willingness to learn. He is teachable. God shows His truths and commandments to people who are teachable. God does not give spiritual understanding to rebels. He gives spiritual understanding to His friends.

In John 15:14-15 Jesus described His friends as those who do whatever He commands them. Jesus promised that He would teach His friends everything He has learned from His Father. God's friends are those who are teachable and obedient. They alone will learn God's message in all of its richness.

Several factors can negatively affect a person's teachable attitude. Mark 4 records a parable Jesus used to identify three different factors that destroy our teachable attitude and keep us from being good Bible students. In the parable Jesus called these factors hard ground (the road), rocky ground, and thorny ground.

Jesus said that some people are like hard soil because their receptivity to God's Word has been destroyed. He said other people are like a thin layer of soil over a shell of rock because different factors have kept them from developing any spiritual depth in which God's Word can take root and grow. He said others are like thorny soil because different factors choke out God's truth in their lives or distract them from it.

The fact that you are engaged in this study indicates that you want your life to be like the fourth group, whose lives are like deep, rich soil that receives the seed of God's Word and produces an abundance of fruit. Identify the roads, the rocky areas, and the thorny areas in your life and begin to pray about them. Doing this may be frightening or frustrating because you do not even know how to begin. Perhaps you have identified these areas in your life and have been struggling with them for a long time—but without much success.

Hebrews 4:15-16 offers encouragement and a promise about your struggle to deal with the factors that try to destroy your teachable attitude. It says that God knows your struggles because in the person of Jesus He experienced those same struggles Himself, and He promises to help you. Go to God without fear or hesitation and claim His promise of help.

Discipline

Discipline in your Bible-study habits is another characteristic that is necessary to create and maintain a spiritual hunger for God's Word.

The best professional athletes train and practice for years to perform their sport in peak condition. The top professional musicians practice for hours each day to develop their ability to its highest level. Bible study also demands discipline and hard work. Christians cannot learn God's truths, commands, and promises by sitting back and expecting the Holy Spirit to program them with truth.

Paul tells Timothy in 2 Timothy 2:15: "Be diligent to present yourself approved to God as a workman who does not need to be ashamed, accurately handling the word of truth." The words in this verse describe hard work and mighty effort. Christians are expected to work hard at developing their ability to interpret and apply God's Word correctly.

A Christian needs a disciplined attitude in order to learn the Bible. There are new words to learn. There are new thoughts about God to understand and apply. The Bible reflects customs we don't practice in our culture. Understanding them is vital to understanding the Bible's message. The Bible speaks about events we haven't heard of before. Understanding them is important in interpreting the Bible. You must be disciplined to be a good Bible student.

A Christian must have discipline in order to maintain the practice of personal Bible study. High school and college students must find time to study the Bible just as they must find time to master history or calculus. Homemakers must find time to study the Bible in addition to cleaning the house and caring for children. Persons who work in business or industry must find time to study the Bible as they face the daily pressures of commuting and carrying a heavy workload. Parents must find time for Bible study in addition to finding time for each other and their children.

You must also have discipline to continue studying the Bible after you begin. Although all parts of the Bible are important, not all parts are equally interesting or clear. Many people have pledged to study and learn the Bible, but they quit as they study some of the books. Some have stopped when they reach Leviticus, and others stumble over Revelation. Although these books are difficult, they are relevant.

You must have the discipline to persevere in order to understand the difficult sections of the Bible. Interpreting the Bible demands skills. It is not just learning a set of inflexible rules. Understanding the Bible requires common sense and sound judgment. These qualities come only from experience. Understanding the Bible demands making choices among different interpretations. This skill requires much experience. To interpret the Bible, you must study diligently.

How to Use This Book

This workbook uses an interactive learning approach that is designed to involve you in the learning process. In addition to reading material about the various topics of study, you will be asked to complete activities that help you practice and apply what you read. Don't neglect this important part of the study. Only by reading the Scriptures and completing the activities can you fully accomplish the goals of understanding and applying the principles of Bible study that are presented.

Each week's study material is divided into five daily lessons. Set apart a definite time and place to complete your daily lesson. Sit down with your Bible, a pencil, this workbook, and any study aids that are recommended for the lesson. Use the material in this workbook to guide your daily study times. Complete only one day's work at a time. Most lessons will require between 40 and 60 minutes. Be consistent in your study time, doing five days of study in this workbook each week.

Consider participating in a group study of this material. If a group study is offered, the group facilitator can use the leader guide beginning on page 207.

In addition to learning how to study the Bible, you will memorize one Scripture verse each week. Memorizing will add to your understanding of scriptural teachings. Remove the Scripture-memory verses from the center of the book, cut them out, and memorize the designated verse each week. Scripture-memory cards are provided for both the *King James Version* and the *New American Standard Bible* so that you may choose the translation from which you prefer to memorize verses.

Here are steps for successful Scripture memorization.

1. *Begin with a positive attitude.* Many think they can't memorize, but Philippians 4:13 says you can do all things through Christ. If you can memorize phone numbers and addresses, you can memorize Scripture.

2. *Glue the reference to the first words.* To remember both the verse and the reference, say the reference and the first words without pausing. For example, "Philippians 4:13—I can do all things."

3. *Memorize bite by bite.* Repeat the verse to the end of the first phrase, ending with the reference. For example, "Philippians 4:13—I can do all things—Philippians 4:13." Say that over and over until you have it memorized. Then repeat what you have learned and add the next phrase, still starting and ending with the reference: "Philippians 4:13—I can do all things through Him—Philippians 4:13" and so on. Memorizing a verse phrase by phrase is easy because you are learning only five or six words at a time. Learn the verse word-perfect this way.

4. *Review, review, review.* This is the master secret to memorization. Use memory cards to review. Say the verse as quickly and accurately as possible. After memorizing, review the verse every day for 90 days, weekly for the next six weeks, then monthly for the rest of your life. The best review is using the verse in your life or to help another person.

5. *Meditate on the verse.* Meditation can increase your grasp of the passage's teaching and its application. Experience Christ as that verse's truth works in you. Think of ways the verse can be lived.

6. *Use spare time wisely.* Carry Scripture-memory cards with you to use during your spare time, such as when exercising or waiting in line.

7. *Team with a friend.* Listen to each other's verse, checking the Bible or Scripture-memory card for accuracy.[1]

Following these seven easy steps will make Scripture memory a meaningful and effective discipline that will enhance your spiritual growth.

Steps for Memorizing Scripture

1. Begin with a positive attitude.
2. Glue the reference to the first words.
3. Memorize bite by bite.
4. Review, review, review.
5. Meditate on the verse.
6. Use spare time wisely.
7. Team with a friend.

Some Books You Will Need

Many lessons in your workbook will refer to Bible-study aids you can use to complete your study. Page 14 includes a list of recommended helpful resources. At the least, make sure you have access to your own Bible dictionary, commentary, and concordance for use in this course. You may want to purchase these to begin your own collection of resources, or you may want to borrow them from your church media library or from a local library. Make a copy of page 14 and use it as a handy guide so you can add to your resource library by acquiring other resources listed.

---

[1]Adapted from Waylon B. Moore, *Living God's Word* (Nashville: LifeWay, 1997), 26–29.

Helpful Resources

Bible Atlas

Brisco, Thomas V. *Holman Bible Atlas.* Nashville: Broadman & Holman, 1999.

Smith, Marsha A. Ellis. *Holman Book of Biblical Charts, Maps, and Reconstructions.* Nashville: Broadman & Holman, 1993.

Bible Culture

Adams, J. McKee. *Biblical Backgrounds.* Nashville: Broadman, 1965.

Bible Dictionary

Butler, Trent C. *Holman Bible Dictionary.* Nashville: Broadman & Holman, 1991.

Bible Encyclopedia

Tenney, Merrill C., ed. *The Zondervan Pictorial Encyclopedia of the Bible.* Grand Rapids: Zondervan, 1975.

Bible Handbook

Dockery, David S. *Holman Bible Handbook.* Nashville: Broadman & Holman, 1992.

Bible History

Kaiser, Walter C., Jr. *A History of Israel.* Nashville: Broadman & Holman, 1998.

Bible Pronunciation

Severance, W. Murray. *That's Easy for You to Say.* Nashville: Broadman & Holman, 1997.

Bible Survey

House, Paul R. *Old Testament Survey.* Nashville: Broadman & Holman, 1997.

Lea, Thomas D. *The New Testament—Its Background and Message.* Nashville: Broadman & Holman, 1996.

Commentary

Anders, Max. *Holman New Testament Commentary.* Nashville: Broadman & Holman, 1998.

Clendenen, E. Ray. *The New American Commentary.* Nashville: Broadman & Holman, 1991.

Shepherd, David R. *Shepherd's Notes.* Nashville: Broadman & Holman, 1997.

Concordance

Strong, James. *Strong's Exhaustive Concordance.* Nashville: Broadman & Holman, 1994.

Topical Bible

Perry, John. *So That's in the Bible.* Nashville: Broadman & Holman, 1997.

Word Studies

Robertson, A. T., and James Swanson. *Word Pictures in the New Testament, Concise Edition.* Nashville: Broadman & Holman, 2000.

Interpreting the Bible is an art and a science. A science has rules and guidelines that describe its content. The interpretation of the Bible requires some guidelines to understand its content. To apply these guidelines demands wisdom and experience, and this is an art. Bible students practice the art of interpretation when they use the right guideline in the right way.

This week you will learn five guidelines to help you interpret the Bible.

Day 1
Understand the Writer's Meaning

The first of the five guidelines, which is highlighted in the box, is the one you will study today. I want to share with you two keys to understanding what the biblical writer meant to say.

Guidelines for Interpreting the Bible

1. **Understand the writer's meaning.**
2. Observe the context.
3. Accept the limits of revelation.
4. Identify the type of writing.
5. Use the Bible to interpret itself.

The first key is to discover the writer's literal meaning. Across the centuries some Bible students have chosen to ignore the literal meaning of a Scripture, looking instead for an allegorical meaning. These students have tried to move from the literal meaning to a deeper spiritual meaning. By taking this approach, these students often read meanings into the Scriptures that the writers never intended.

The Bible does have deep spiritual meanings, but a serious Bible student's goal is to begin by discovering what the writer was trying to say.

The other key to understanding the writer's meaning is to understand figures of speech. A passage of Scripture might have

Week 1

Guidelines for Interpreting the Bible

Day 1
Understand the Writer's Meaning

Day 2
Observe the Context

Day 3
Accept the Limits of Revelation

Day 4
Identify the Type of Writing

Day 5
Use the Bible to Interpret Itself

SCRIPTURE-MEMORY VERSE
Be kind to one another, tender-hearted, forgiving each other, just as God in Christ also has forgiven you.
Ephesians 4:32

some elements you cannot interpret literally. Psalm 91:4 describes God with these words: "He shall cover thee with his feathers, and under his wings shalt thou trust" (KJV). If we take the literal meaning, should you conclude that God has feathers and wings? No, because the psalmist is using a figure of speech called a metaphor. A metaphor uses one object in place of another to suggest a likeness between them.

To understand the verse's intended meaning, you must seek the meaning of the figure of speech. The language used describes the way a hen covers her chicks with feathers and wings. God doesn't have feathers and wings, but He does have love and is strong. The psalmist used the metaphor to describe the Father's love and protection. Because poetic writings like Psalms often employ figures of speech, we should be alert for these figures as we read poetic books and passages in the Bible.

Now I want you to work with some figures of speech. A commentary will be helpful, or you may want to talk with your pastor or another experienced Bible student.

† Study each passage listed in the left column on the following chart. Then write in the middle column what you think the writer meant. (Leave the Applications column blank for now.)

Passage	The Writer's Meaning	Applications
Psalm 119:105	_____	_____
Matthew 7:3-4	_____	_____
Mark 9:33-37	_____	_____

When you interpret the Bible, look for the normal, obvious meaning. This is the literal meaning. A passage of Scripture will have only one literal meaning. We may disagree over what the literal meaning actually is, but only one of the possible meanings can be correct.

Even though a passage has only one literal meaning, it may have many possible applications. The application is the way you use the passage in daily life.

† Now go back to the chart. Based on your understanding of the writer's meaning in each passage, write one way to apply each passage to your life.

Read Ephesians 4:32. Notice what it teaches about the motivation behind forgiveness. List different situations in which you might apply this passage to your life.

_____

_____

Ephesians 4:32 is your Scripture-memory verse for this week. Begin memorizing it by using the Scripture-memory card at the center of your workbook.

Day 2
Observe the Context

This week you are learning five guidelines for accurately interpreting the Bible. Yesterday you learned to understand the writer's meaning by interpreting the Bible literally and by interpreting figures of speech. You also learned that a given passage of Scripture has one meaning but many possible applications.

Today you will study another important guideline for Bible interpretation, highlighted in the box below.

Guidelines for Interpreting the Bible

1. Understand the writer's meaning.
2. **Observe the context.**
3. Accept the limits of revelation.
4. Identify the type of writing.
5. Use the Bible to interpret itself.

The second guideline for interpreting the Bible is to observe the context. One part of the context is the biblical context—the section in the Bible where a given verse or passage appears. The biblical context of a statement or verse refers to the verses surrounding the statement. It may also refer to the context of an entire book of the Bible. This wider context is sometimes crucial in understanding a passage's meaning.

To understand the importance of biblical context, read John 9:3. Notice Jesus' startling statement " 'neither that this man sinned, nor his parents.' " Could this "sinless" man be descended from a "sinless" family? To understand verse 3, you must read it in context with verses 1 and 2.

---

† Consider John 9:3 in context and write what you think Jesus was saying when He made this statement.

_____

_____

In this context Jesus was not discussing the subject of sinlessness either at birth or in life. He was discussing whether the man's blindness was caused by somebody's sin. Jesus said that the man's blindness was caused by neither his own sin nor that of his parents. A closer reading of the surrounding verses can prevent a serious misunderstanding of Scripture.

Let's look at another passage. In Luke 14:26 Jesus said that you cannot be His disciple unless you hate your parents and your children and all the other persons who are dear to you. Could that possibly be true?

---

† Read Luke 14:15-35 to see verse 26 in context. Then write what you think Jesus was saying in that verse.

_____

_____

When Jesus spoke these words, He was on the way to the cross. He was trying to emphasize to His followers in the most vivid terms possible the degree of devotion that discipleship demands and the importance of counting the cost of discipleship. No other love in life must compare to our love for Him.

The context of the Bible also refers to the culture or circumstances in which a given event or statement appears. A knowledge of biblical social customs, history, and geography can greatly help you interpret the Bible. A knowledge of the circumstances under which a writer wrote can illuminate his message. You will need help discovering a passage's social and cultural context. A commentary, a New Testament survey or introduction, and a Bible dictionary are helpful for understanding the context of a verse.

Read Paul's joy-filled words in Philippians 4:4: "Rejoice in the Lord always; again I will say, rejoice!" What makes this exhortation from Paul special? Let's discover where Paul was and the conditions under which he was living when he wrote Philippians 4:4.

✝ Check the biblical context of Philippians 4:4 to see if you can find evidence of Paul's circumstances when he wrote that verse. Check the correct response.
❑ On his way to visit the Philippians
❑ In King Agrippa's palace
❑ In prison
❑ On the banks of the Jordan River

Paul was not living under the best conditions when he wrote this, was he? Paul's reference to the "guard" and his "imprisonment" in Philippians 1:13 suggests that he was under arrest.

✝ Now use a commentary, a New Testament survey, or a Bible dictionary to learn more about Paul's circumstances when he wrote the Book of Philippians. Write some of your findings. Use the margin if you need more space.

When Paul urged his readers to express their joy, his circumstances were not easy. He was under arrest and confined. Perhaps Paul's situation was not solitary confinement, but he was likely chained to a guard and confined to his own house (see Acts 28:30). Knowing the biblical and cultural context suggests to contemporary Christians that if Paul could be joyful in this situation, God's strength must be unbelievable! A knowledge of Paul's situation adds a meaningful dimension to this passage.

Through the parable of the Good Samaritan in Luke 10:30-37, Jesus spoke to a prominent Jew who felt that he was one of God's favored people. In the parable a priest and a Levite refuse to help the wounded man. Stopping would inconvenience them. Only the Samaritan sacrificed himself for the wounded man. What was special about this act of mercy?

✝ **Use one or more of the Bible-study tools you used previously to discover the cultural context of Luke 10:30-37. Write your explanation. Use the margin if you need more space.**

_____

_____

To fully understand the impact of this story on the Jews of Jesus' time, we must know how they viewed the Samaritans. The Samaritans were a mixed-race people who practiced a religion with a combination of Judaism and paganism. The Jews hated them. It was unthinkable to a Jew that a Samaritan would show the mercy Jesus described. The average Jew would not want this mercy from a Samaritan.

✝ **Why do you think Jesus characterized the Samaritan this way?**

_____

_____

When you know the context of this verse in the life of the Jewish people, its meaning becomes clear and understandable in your own time. Jesus pointedly challenged the Jews' prejudice and arrogance by characterizing the Samaritan as merciful and compassionate.

As you read your Bible this week, be especially sensitive to the way the context of the verses can increase your understanding.

Day 3
Accept the Limits of Revelation

Recall that this week you are studying guidelines for interpreting the Bible. You have already studied and practiced using two of those guidelines.

† **Try to recall the guidelines you have learned so far this week by filling in the blanks.**

1. **Understand the writer's** _____.

2. **Observe the** _____.

Check your responses against the correct guidelines listed in the following box. You will also see highlighted the guideline you will study today.

Guidelines for Interpreting the Bible

1. Understand the writer's meaning.
2. Observe the context.
3. **Accept the limits of revelation.**
4. Identify the type of writing.
5. Use the Bible to interpret itself.

Where God has spoken in the Bible, He has spoken accurately and truthfully. However, the Bible has not spoken on all subjects of interest to us. Sometimes a Bible student attempts to strain from the Bible more information than God has placed there.

The Bible's primary purpose is to outline God's plan for our redemption through Christ. The Bible is not a textbook of medicine or science. The Bible is not concerned with predicting the arrival of spaceships or answering every question about the way the world will end. Remember the primary purpose of the Bible as you seek to understand its meaning.

Even when the Bible speaks about our redemption and other topics of spiritual interest, God has not told us all we may want to know. He has shared in the Bible all that is necessary for our spiritual needs. We must be content with this information and not try to push beyond it.

If you are like me, you still have quite a few questions for which you would like to be able to find biblical answers. And if you are like me, you have not yet found answers that are completely satisfactory.

✝ **What are some questions you wish the Bible answered? Write them in or around the question mark below.**

One of the most widespread promises in Scripture is that Jesus Christ will return again bodily. Such passages as Titus 2:12-13 and 1 Thessalonians 4:13-18 gloriously describe this event. However, the Bible has not provided a clear outline of the chronology of Jesus' return.

✝ Read Mark 13:32 and check what Jesus said about the precise time of His return.
❑ Jesus would decide at a later time.
❑ Jesus knew the answer but refused to tell.
❑ The angels would vote on a good time for Jesus to return.
❑ Only God knew the time of Jesus' return.

Mark 13:32 shows that even Jesus Himself did not know the exact hour of His return when He spoke these words; only God knew. A verse like this should warn us against predicting that Jesus will come in our lifetime. It should warn us against rigidly arranging the events that will occur when Jesus returns. We must not view our opinion as God's final word on the subject.

Likewise, the Bible also does not describe all of the reasons for tragedy and suffering. It is spiritually unwise to use Scripture to prove God's purposes in allowing a given event in someone's life.

✝ Read 2 Corinthians 12:7-10. Why did Paul say that God allowed a "thorn in the flesh" to plague him?
❑ To destroy his self-esteem
❑ To teach him dependence on God
❑ To teach him the consequences of disobedience
❑ To make him miserable

Paul learned that God had permitted his "thorn in the flesh" to teach him more complete dependence on the Lord (see 2 Corinthians 12:9-10). However, this personal assurance was intended for and given specifically to Paul. The cause of much suffering is a mystery. Although we can be certain that God's strength empowers us to endure suffering (see James 1:2-4), we must be careful in using the Bible to show a suffering Christian what God is trying to do in his life.

Sometimes the teaching about the relationship of Christian wives to their husbands is distorted by the misuse of the Bible. Some have used the Bible to suggest that a Christian wife must always follow her husband even if it leads to sin, disobedience, or away from the church.

†Read 1 Peter 3:1. What reason did Peter give for wives to submit to their husbands?
❑ To teach them a lesson
❑ To make them feel guilty
❑ To win them to Christ
❑ To learn humility

Peter urged wives to submit themselves to their husbands specifically for the purpose of winning them to Christ. Peter was not talking about absolute obedience to an overbearing husband. He was describing how a Christian wife may influence her non-Christian husband to see Christ's character in her. It would be going beyond the Bible's meaning to suggest that the Bible teaches that the wife must obey the husband even if it leads her to disobey God. Peter had an entirely different purpose in mind, outlining a way to win a stubborn non-Christian husband to Christ. We must not press the Bible to say more than God has spoken.

Cultivate the ability to be content to know only what God wants you to know. Serious Bible students do not find it necessary to demand from the Bible answers that it does not provide. Rather, they accept the limits of revelation.

†By now you should have memorized this week's Scripture-memory verse. Write the verse from memory.

_____

_____

_____

_____

Now recite the verse aloud. If another person is available, ask that person to use your Scripture-memory card to check you.

Day 4
Identify the Type of Writing

Today you will learn a new guideline for interpreting the Bible. It is the fourth guideline highlighted below.

Guidelines for Interpreting the Bible

1. Understand the writer's meaning.
2. Observe the context.
3. Accept the limits of revelation.
4. **Identify the type of writing.**
5. Use the Bible to interpret itself.

The Bible contains many different types of writing. Accurately interpreting the Bible requires knowing what kind of literature you are reading.

✝ **Without doing any research or looking at the illustration on page 26, label each of the following books of the Bible according to the primary type of writing you think it represents: poetry, prophecy, narrative, or letter.**

Genesis	_____	Acts	_____
Exodus	_____	Galatians	_____
Psalms	_____	1 and 2 Timothy	_____
Proverbs	_____	Hebrews	_____
Daniel	_____	Jude	_____
The Gospels	_____	Revelation	_____

Some of biblical literature is Hebrew poetry. The Books of Psalms, Proverbs, and many of the Old Testament Prophets contain poetry. Writings of prophecy give a glimpse of what God will do in the future. The Old Testament Book of Daniel and the New Testament Book of Revelation are examples of prophetic writings. Narrative writings give accounts of what God has done in history. Genesis and Exodus in the Old Testament and the

Gospels (Matthew, Mark, Luke, and John) and Acts in the New Testament are narratives. The New Testament also has letters from Paul, Peter, and John. Letters like Galatians, 1 and 2 Timothy, Hebrews, Jude, and many others teach God's message to young Christians. They are called epistles.

Some books of the Bible have several kinds of writing in the same book. Isaiah, for example, has poetry, prophecy, and narrative sections. However, each book fits primarily into one category, although it may contain elements of other kinds of writings. The bookcase illustration below will help you identify the primary classification of the writings in each book of the Bible.

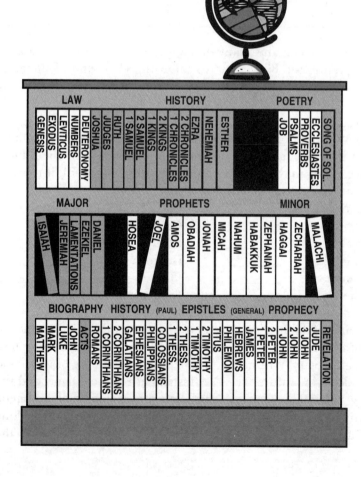

To interpret the Bible properly, it is important to observe the kind of writing you are reading. Poetry and prophecy use many figures of speech. You have already learned that you must be alert to figures of speech, such as metaphors, and you must take care to understand what the writer is saying. If you have not added a commentary to your Bible-study tools, I hope you plan to do so soon. You really need one to help you with the following exercises. Let's look now at some figures of speech in the Bible and practice discovering what the writer was actually saying.

Isaiah 1:16 is a portion of Hebrew poetry. Most versions of the Bible designate poetry by setting off the words in poetic form. Notice the context of Isaiah's words. The prophet has described the rebellion of the children of Israel. Their prayers were empty. The people had turned against God.

✝ **Read Isaiah 1:16. What does Isaiah say the solution is?**

_____

_____

The Scripture says the people should wash themselves and make themselves clean. Are a bathtub and a bar of soap the solutions for the guilt of sin? Surely not! This must be a figure of speech.

✝ **Use a commentary to discover what the writer means in Isaiah 1:16. Then write your interpretation. Use the margin if you need more space.**

_____

_____

The figure of speech in Isaiah 1:16 calls for repentance, spiritual cleansing, and fresh commitment to God. This cleansing does not require soap and water. It demands confessing and forsaking sin.

In Revelation 13:1, John pictures a wild beast who leads human beings into evil.

✝ **Read Revelation 13:1. Without doing any investigation, check what you think is the correct identity of the beast.**
❑ **A wild animal like one you might see in a zoo**
❑ **A symbol for the evil power of the Roman Empire**
❑ **An evil human being in the last times**

We are safe to say that this is not a zoo animal. It is harder to choose between the other two options. Here it would be helpful to read a commentary on Revelation 13:1 to gain understanding. This is a prophetic passage, and the beast is a symbol. You probably need help to understand what the symbol means.

✝ **Study the commentary again and write a brief interpretation of the beast in Revelation 13:1.**

_____

_____

Acts 3:7 appears in the form of a narrative passage. Luke, the writer of Acts, describes Peter healing a man who had been lame from birth. Peter healed him in the presence of a crowd of people.

✝ **Read Acts 3:7. Because Acts is narrative writing, how should we interpret the incident described?**
❑ **Literally**   ❑ **Symbolically**   ❑ **Allegorically**

Luke intended that we understand this as a literal miracle. It doesn't mean Peter touched the man and so inspired him with positive thinking that he could get up and walk on his own. Nor does the account merely represent the spiritual healing God can bring to our lives. By the power of Jesus Christ, Peter performed a miracle on a man who was genuinely lame. This is narrative writing. Make a simple, literal interpretation of this type of writing.

Although the narrative books and the epistles are to be taken more literally than prophecy and poetry, these books also contain occasional figures of speech that must be interpreted. Colossians is a letter from Paul to the church at Colossae asking for prayer for his work. Do you see a figure of speech in chapter 4, verse 3?

✝ **Read Colossians 4:3 and identify the figure of speech. Decide how it should be interpreted, and write your answer here.**

_____

_____

_____

The figure of speech is the word *door*, and it represents an opportunity to preach Christ. Paul asked his readers to pray that God would provide him an opportunity to preach Christ.

When you read the Bible, observe the kind of writing you read. If the writing is poetry or prophecy, be alert to interpret properly the many figures of speech. If the writing is narrative or a letter, interpret the writing more literally.

Day 5
Use the Bible to Interpret Itself

Today you will study the fifth guideline for interpreting the Bible.

Guidelines for Interpreting the Bible

1. Understand the writer's meaning.
2. Observe the context.
3. Accept the limits of revelation.
4. Identify the type of writing.
5. Use the Bible to interpret itself.

Many passages in the Bible are not easy to understand. Often these difficult passages become clearer when you use another passage of the Bible to help explain them. You can use the Bible to explain itself by allowing a clearer passage to help clarify a more obscure passage.

Many subjects in the Bible are discussed in more than one passage of the Bible. Sometimes the Bible discusses a subject briefly in one section and more fully in another section. Always use the more detailed discussion as you seek to understand the Bible.

It is true that one mention of a truth or a commandment in the Bible is enough to make it important. However, the intent of that one reference may not be clear. In this case you shouldn't use the unclear passage to glean firm doctrine. In 1 Corinthians 15:29 Paul referred to those who "are baptized for the dead." This phrase seems to suggest that one person can be baptized for another person. Such an idea, however, would contradict other biblical teachings on baptism (see Acts 8:36; 1 Peter 3:21), which always picture baptism as an experience Christians undergo to express their own faith in Christ. The exact meaning of this passage is not clear. We can be sure, however, that it does not suggest proxy baptism, because such a meaning would contradict other passages in the Bible.

To understand important doctrine and teachings, it is best to use Bible passages that fully discuss the doctrine. For example, the resurrection of Christ is fully discussed in 1 Corinthians 15. The nature of faith is discussed in Hebrews 11. It is important to use all of these passages in studies of these subjects.

Getting a complete picture of the biblical teaching on a subject is another important way to use the Bible to interpret itself. A careless reading of Matthew 21:22 may lead a person to believe that he can get anything he wants from God if he has enough faith. But hold on a minute! Let's learn how other passages illuminate the meaning of this verse.

✝ First read Matthew 21:22. Then read John 14:13; James 4:3; and 1 John 5:14-15. On page 31 write a brief summary of what these passages teach that helps you interpret Matthew 21:22.

John 14:13 _____

_____

_____

James 4:3 _____

_____

_____

1 John 5:14-15 _____

_____

_____

James 4:3 shows you that God will not answer prayer if your motive is selfish. God says in 1 John 5:14-15 that His will is the important factor in receiving an answer to prayer. Faith alone will not guarantee that God will grant a request. Some of these requests might not be in God's will. John 14:13 states the same truth. When you pray, you must seek God's will and not your own wishes.

Matthew 21:22 shows the importance of faith in God in receiving an answer to prayer. It does not teach that you can get anything from God if you only believe. You must be concerned with obedience to God, a desire for God's will, and good motives if you want God to answer your prayers.

When you want to understand what the Bible teaches on a particular subject, consider all biblical teachings on the subject. If you limit your study to a single passage, you might reach a wrong conclusion. Use the Bible to interpret itself. It is its own best interpreter.

This week you learned five guidelines for interpreting Scripture. Begin putting these into practice in your Bible study. By helping you interpret the Bible accurately, these guidelines will help you gain a deeper understanding of what you read, as well as enjoy the rich blessings God intended you to receive from His Word.

† Review what you have learned this week by filling in the blanks.

1. Understand the writer's _____.

2. Observe the _____.

3. Accept the limits of _____.

4. Identify the type of _____.

5. Use the Bible to _____ itself.

If you had difficulty listing the guidelines, take a moment to review.

† Write from memory your Scripture-memory verse for this week.

_____

_____

_____

_____

Describe one way this verse has changed your thinking or behavior this week.

_____

_____

† Close your week's study with prayer. Thank God for His Word and ask Him to guide you through this study. Commit to God to do your best and to maintain a teachable attitude.

Last week you learned five guidelines for helping you accurately read and interpret God's Word. When you understand what Bible passages mean, you then need to apply them to daily life. This week you will learn principles to help you apply the Bible to your everyday experiences. Here are the five principles you will study.

Principles for Applying the Bible

1. Apply the Bible according to its real meaning.
2. Use the Bible as a Book of principles.
3. Use the promises properly.
4. Use a cross-cultural understanding.
5. Use the Bible wisely.

Day 1
Apply the Bible According to Its Real Meaning

A group of young Christians from an Ethiopian tribe was visiting in a missionary home. One of the missionary's children bounded into the living room, with the family dog right behind. When the small dog approached the Ethiopian visitors in a friendly fashion, the guests retreated in apparent fear.

Assuming they were afraid, the missionary assured them that the dog wouldn't harm them. The guests replied that they were not fearful. Rather, they believed that Christians were not to have dogs around them. Their biblical support for this belief was Paul's word to "beware of dogs" (Philippians 3:2, KJV). The missionary explained that Paul had nothing against dogs; he was referring to human beings who acted like dirty, vicious street dogs.[1] The zealous young Christians had applied a verse in their lives but had given it the wrong meaning.

Whenever you apply a verse to your life, you must use it in accordance with its real meaning. A Bible student's first goal is to learn what the verse means. Only then can you apply it to life based on what that verse really means. Many Bible verses can be

Week 2

Principles for Applying the Bible

Day 1
Apply the Bible According to Its Real Meaning

Day 2
Use the Bible as a Book of Principles

Day 3
Use the Promises Properly

Day 4
Use a Cross-Cultural Understanding

Day 5
Use the Bible Wisely

Scripture-Memory Verse
Casting all your anxiety upon Him, because He cares for you.
1 Peter 5:7

misapplied by readers who do not understand the verses' real meanings. In this session you will practice reading several verses, discovering the real meaning of each verse, and writing ways you can apply those verses to your life based on their real meanings. Contemporary Bible translations and a commentary will help you complete the following activities.

---

† Read Ephesians 4:26. Use Bible translations and a commentary to discover the real meaning of this verse. Check the statement that most accurately summarizes it.
❑ Practice being angry so that you are angry all the time.
❑ Express your anger before sundown.
❑ You will get angry, but don't let it get out of control and lead you into sin.

Paul recognized the reality of righteous anger. People become indignant over their own treatment or the treatment of others. It might be wrong not to be indignant. It would also be wrong to allow the indignation to escalate until it is out of control. Indignation over wrong might lead to action based on wounded pride or personal resentment. This would be sinful. Paul is saying to you: "If you get angry, don't let your anger lead you into sinful acts. Keep your anger under control." Knowing the meaning of the verse helps you apply it.

---

† Write a way to apply Ephesians 4:26 to your life.

_____

_____

_____

Only you and God know the way you need to apply this verse about anger. Maybe you need to pray about losing your temper. Maybe you need to acknowledge your anger and seek healthy ways to express and resolve it. Maybe you would like to apologize to someone you have hurt because of anger.

✝ Read 1 Thessalonians 5:17. Using various translations and a commentary, discover the real meaning of the verse. Check the statement that most accurately expresses it.

❑ Remain in an attitude of prayer at all times.
❑ Pray all the time without taking a break—even for eating, sleeping, and reading the Bible.
❑ You should feel guilty when you are not praying.

You should have discovered that to pray without ceasing means that you should be continually in an attitude of prayer. Paul does not mean that you should pray so that you never eat, sleep, or read the Bible. He wants an attitude of prayer to be constantly within you. He doesn't want you to feel guilty if you are not praying. Other actions in the Christian life besides prayer are also important.

✝ Write a way to apply 1 Thessalonians 5:17 to your life.

_____

_____

Perhaps this verse made you realize that you can remain in an attitude of prayer all day long, no matter what you are doing. Maybe you decided to be more intentional about calling on God and praising Him as you go through each day. Or did you decide that certain thoughts and actions are inappropriate for someone who remains in a continual attitude of prayer?

✝ Read 1 Timothy 5:23. Read Bible translations and a commentary to discover the real meaning of the verse. Then check the statement that best conveys that meaning.

❑ Stop drinking water altogether.
❑ It is OK for believers to drink alcoholic beverages.
❑ Timothy should drink a small amount of wine for medicinal purposes.

To understand what Paul means, consider both the water conditions and the purpose for drinking the wine. Water in Paul's day was often impure. Drinking only that water could make Timothy sick. Wine in Paul's day could be used as a medicine, and that is the purpose Paul had in mind. He was not telling Timothy to use wine as a beverage but as a medicine to treat his stomach problems.

✝ How can you apply 1 Timothy 5:23 to your life?

_____

_____

_____

Today healthful water and effective medicines make unnecessary the drinking of wine for these purposes. However, this verse may have reminded you to eliminate a food from your diet that is causing you digestive problems or to discontinue the use of another substance that is not good for you.

✝ Read 1 Peter 3:6. Using various translations and a commentary, discover the real meaning of the verse. Check the statement that best summarizes that meaning.
❑ A Christian wife should view her husband as an army private views his company commander.
❑ A wife should respectfully obey her husband.
❑ A wife should worship her husband as her lord.

You probably discovered that Peter spoke of the respect a husband and a wife should have for each other. Such respect will lead the wife to respectfully hear and follow the husband's suggestions. Peter's purpose was to commend Sarah's respect for Abraham. He didn't intend for Sarah or a modern wife to treat her husband like a field marshall. Notice that Peter urged the husband to give the same respect to the wife in verse 7.

✝ Write a way you can apply 1 Peter 3:6 or 7 to your life.

_____

_____

A wife might apply this verse by asking God to help her develop a "gentle and quiet spirit" (v. 4) and to help her realize her husband's godly qualities. She might decide to submit to his leadership in ways she has been unwilling to before. A husband can apply verse 7 by praying that God will make him a man worthy of his wife's respect as the spiritual leader of the home. Perhaps he will think of ways to be understanding of and sensitive to his wife's needs in ways he hasn't before.

✝ Make time each day to review last week's Scripture-memory verse to keep it in your mental memory bank. Also begin memorizing this week's memory verse, 1 Peter 5:7. Use the appropriate Scripture-memory card at the center of your workbook.

_____

[1] Raymond Davis, _Fire on the Mountains_ (Toronto: SIM International, 1980), 112.

Day 2
Use the Bible as a Book of Principles

This week you are learning five principles for effectively applying the Bible to your life.

✝ Recall the first principle, which you learned yesterday, or find it in day 1 and fill in the blank. Notice the second principle, which you will study today.

1. Apply the Bible according to its real _____.
2. Use the Bible as a Book of principles.

The Bible contains many principles that show you how to live for and serve God. The Bible warns you against many acts and attitudes that hinder your life and service for God. The directions and guidelines the Bible gives are often not detailed and specific. They are usually general and broad.

If the Bible were too specific in its warnings, it would be limited to one time and culture. If the Bible were a group of specific rules for every occasion, you might obey the letter of the rules and miss the genuine spirit of godly living. God intends that you struggle to discern the way He wants you to apply His principles to your life. That way you stay focused on developing a deeper relationship with Him through which He directs your thoughts and actions and teaches you how to apply His Word.

† Read Acts 2:42-45. Luke, the author of Acts, describes Christians who sold their private belongings and gave them to Christian friends. Should we do the same today? Do you think we are to infer from this passage that it is wrong for a Christian to own private property? ❏ Yes ❏ No Read a commentary to find the answer.

First, notice that in his narrative account Luke did not command us to copy what these early Christians did. He presented their examples, but he didn't command us to imitate them. Also, do you remember the principle of using the Bible to interpret itself? No other passages in the Bible command Christians to sell their property and give it to the poor, although many passages call on Christians to be unselfish and generous (see James 5:1-5; 1 John 3:17).

This spirit of generosity Luke described was due to the great sense of unity the Holy Spirit had produced in the church. The rich members made provision for the poorer members from their wealth. For a brief time no one could complain of hunger or general need. When the sense of unity waned, some Christians pretended to share their goods but actually did not (see Acts 5:1-11). Nothing is wrong with owning property. However, we must be generous and avoid hypocrisy about our generosity.

✝ **What principle can we draw from Acts 2:42-45?**

_____

_____

_____

Luke depicted the generosity and unselfishness of the early church. He did not command that we sell our private property or feel guilty for owning private goods. He reminded us that we must be eager to share with the needy.

✝ **Read 1 Corinthians 8:13. Paul said that he would stop eating meat if that offended his fellow Christians. What has meat to do with the Christian life? Do you think Paul is teaching that it is wrong for us to eat meat?** ❑ Yes ❑ No **Read a commentary to explore the issue Paul faced.**

Early Christians could purchase meat to eat from an idol temple in their city. This meat had been part of a sacrifice to a pagan god. The unburned part of the sacrifice could be sold for eating. The meat was reasonable in price and tasty.

This practice offended some Christians because they felt that eating this meat was sinful. They didn't eat it, and they didn't want others to eat it. If they saw Paul eating such meat, his example would harm them. Paul knew all of this and decided not to eat meat.

✝ **What principle can we draw from 1 Corinthians 8:13?**

_____

_____

_____

Paul would not do anything that harmed the spiritual life of another Christian. Eating meat in itself is not wrong. However, if any action harms another Christian, you should avoid it. That is the way you can apply Paul's principle today.

† Read James 2:1-7. Read a commentary to understand the problem James was discussing.

The Christians in James 2 were giving rich people the best seats in their meetings and telling the poor to find their own seats on the floor. It was a clear sense of bias against the poor and toward the rich. James called this sin.

† What principle can we draw from James 2:1-7?

_____

_____

James stated the principle that Christians must not be biased for the rich and against the poor.

When you have found broad, general directions and guidelines in the Bible, you can derive principles for Christian living from them. Let's practice doing that.

† Study Mark 9:33-37. Draw several general principles from those verses and write them here and in the margin.

_____

_____

† Beside the following statements, write A if your principles agree with the statement; write D if your principles disagree; write a question mark if you are not sure.

___ 1. We should value people primarily because of what they can do for us.

___ 2. Ambition and the desire to achieve are inconsistent with a Christian lifestyle.

___ 3. True greatness is in how much we serve, not in how much we are served.

___ 4. Jesus loves children more than He loves adults.
___ 5. When we serve others, we honor ourselves.
___ 6. A concern for self and a concern for serving others
     are inconsistent values in the life of a Christian.

You probably agreed with statements 2, 3, and 6.

The Bible provides broad principles and guidelines that Christians should follow. To apply the Bible accurately, identify and apply the principles the Bible teaches.

Day 3
Use the Promises Properly

Your study this week focuses on principles for applying the Bible. Take a moment to review what you have learned so far.

✝ **Fill in the blanks to complete the principles you have learned this week, looking back to previous lessons if you need to. You will study the third principle today.**

1. Apply the Bible according to its real _____.
2. Use the Bible as a Book of _____.
3. Use the promises properly.

"Every promise of the Bible is mine." Have you heard someone say that? It is not true. There are at least four different kinds of promises in the Bible. When you encounter any promise in the Bible, you must be careful to understand what kind of promise it is, and you must exercise caution in how you apply that promise to your life or to the lives of others. Let's look at these promises.

Types of Bible Promises

- Universal promises
- Promises limited to God's people
- Personal promises
- Conditional promises

Some promises are universal. Some promises in the Bible apply equally to all people.

✝ Read John 3:16. To whom does this promise apply?

_____

This promise is made to all believers. General appeals to trust Christ, like John 3:16, are intended for all people.

Some promises are limited to God's people. Some promises may appear to offer comfort to those who are not Christians, but they apply in their fullest sense to Christians.

✝ Your Scripture-memory verse for this week, 1 Peter 5:7, is a promise with a related exhortation. You should have memorized this verse by now. Try writing it from memory.

_____

_____

This promise is the key to overcoming worries that can defeat you. Peter urged his readers to cast all their concerns on God. God's care for them was the encouragement to do this. These words sound good to use with all people. However, they best apply to committed Christians. God's children can trust their worries to their Heavenly Father. Unbelievers lack the relationship needed to enjoy the command.

Some promises are personal—intended for one specific person or group. Promises to any individual or group are not always for general use.

✝ Read Joshua 1:9. To whom did God speak these words?

_____

God spoke the words of Joshua 1:9 to Joshua alone. This mighty general was about to lead the children of Israel into the Promised Land. A series of mighty battles lay ahead. Joshua and his people needed God's encouragement for the struggle. God promised to be with them. Soldiers entering battle today can hope for God's presence with their cause, but they cannot expect God to act as He did with Joshua.

Some promises are conditional. A conditional promise is good only if the person to whom the promise is made meets a condition specified with the promise.

✝ Read James 4:8. What is the condition that must be met?

_____

Read 1 Peter 5:6. What is the condition that must be met?

_____

James wrote that God comes near to those who seek Him. In the same way, 1 Peter 5:6 contains a condition. God will exalt or glorify us only if we humble ourselves under the circumstances He sends into our lives. Experiencing the promise depends on fulfilling God's condition.

We want to give you some Bible promises to file away for future use, but it is important that you file them properly so that you can use them properly in the future.

✝ Study each promise in the following list. Then list that promise on one of the folders illustrated on page 44. We have filed a few to get you started.

John 3:16	2 Chronicles 7:14	Exodus 4:12
Joshua 1:9	John 15:26	Jeremiah 11:4b
John 14:6	1 Peter 5:7	Luke 1:20
Hebrews 13:5	James 4:8	Micah 4:3

UNIVERSAL

CONTENTS
1. JOHN 3: 16

2. _____

3. _____

LIMITED

CONTENTS
1. 1 PETER 5: 7

2. _____

3. _____

PERSONAL

CONTENTS
1. JOSHUA 1: 9

2. _____

3. _____

CONDITIONAL

CONTENTS
1. JAMES 4: 8

2. _____

3. _____

I hope you found it easy to classify the promises. John 3:16; John 14:6; and Micah 4:3 are universal promises. First Peter 5:7; Hebrews 13:5; and John 15:26 are limited to believers. Joshua 1:9; Luke 1:20; and Exodus 4:12 are personal promises. James 4:8; 2 Chronicles 7:14; and Jeremiah 11:4b are conditional promises.

Sincere Christians can abuse Bible promises when they seek God's guidance by opening His Word without regard to the content of the book they read. They may take the first verse they discover as God's specific message to them. They may run the risk of finding a verse like Colossians 3:5, which says, "Consider the members of your earthly body as dead." They may also find a verse like Deuteronomy 33:8: "Let thy Thummim and thy Urim be with thy holy one" (KJV). Taken as personal promises, the first verse is misleading, and the second is confusing.

Sometimes sincere Christians become concerned about the physical condition of a friend or loved one. In asking God to heal a sick friend, they may use a verse like James 5:15, which promises health for a prayer offered in faith. They should use other passages of Scripture to understand James 5:15. Remember that 1 John 5:14-15 shows that God's will is the most important factor in prayer. Although God's will is generally for health, it is not true that all sick people get well.

Sincere Christians must wisely use Bible promises and not abuse them. The way Bible promises are applied in life depends on whether they are universal, limited to God's people, personal, or conditional.

Day 4
Use a Cross-Cultural Understanding

So far this week you have learned three of five principles for applying the Bible to your life. Complete the following review and notice the principle you will learn today.

✝ **Fill in the blanks at the top of page 46 to name the first three principles for correctly applying the Bible.**

1. Apply the Bible according to its real _____.
2. Use the Bible as a Book of _____.
3. Use the _____ properly.
4. Use a cross-cultural understanding.

Some of the Bible's commands and directions seem confusing today because they are based on the culture of the Bible. Yet the biblical command reveals an important principle or truth we can practice today if we modify the form in which we practice it. This technique again shows that the Bible is a Book of principles rather than a catalog of specific rules and laws.

† Read 2 Corinthians 13:12. What did Paul tell these early believers to do?

_____

Paul urged his readers to "greet one another with a holy kiss." If Christian men and women in churches today greeted one another with holy kisses, we might misunderstand their actions. To say the least, their actions would make most of us uncomfortable. However, there is a principle or truth here that we can apply to our lives.

† What is the principle in 2 Corinthians 13:12, and how can we apply it today?

_____

_____

_____

Paul urged his readers to show deep brotherly love for one another. We can show brotherly love with a warm, firm handshake. By replacing the kiss with a handshake or even a warm embrace, we have demonstrated the principle of brotherly love.

† Read 1 Peter 2:18. What did Peter tell slaves to do?

_____

_____

Peter directed slaves to submit themselves to their masters with all respect. Can we infer from this that we have permission from Peter to own slaves? Of course not! But there is a principle or truth.

† What is the principle in 1 Peter 2:18, and how can we apply it today?

_____

_____

_____

Peter was not approving slavery in this verse. However, he accepted the fact that slavery was a part of his culture and that some very fine Christians were slaves. The principle here is that an employee should respect and work hard for his employer. When an employee today practices honesty and appreciation for his employer, he follows Peter's command.

† Read John 13:1-17. What did Jesus do for the disciples?

_____

_____

These verses record that Jesus washed His disciples' feet and urged them to wash one another's feet. Should Christians accept this incident as a biblical example that should be followed today? Not necessarily. But there is a principle we can apply to our lives.

✝ What is the principle in John 13:1-17, and how can we apply it today?

_____

_____

_____

Foot washing in Jesus' day was usually done by a servant. Jesus and His disciples were meeting in the upper room for the Last Supper. When they came in from the street, they needed to have the dust and grime of the road washed from their feet. There was no servant to do this. Jesus became a servant and did it for His disciples.

Even though we do not need to practice the same act of foot washing today, we need to show the same practice of meekness and humility by serving others. We may apologize to someone we have hurt, or we may take a meal to a home in a time of sickness. These are modern examples of washing feet.

All of the Old Testament commands are not binding on us today. For example, the ritual commands about offering sacrifices (see Leviticus 1–7) and eating certain foods (see Leviticus 11) are not spiritually important today.

✝ Read Hebrews 10:14. Why are the ritual commands no longer binding on believers? Write your answer.

_____

_____

Hebrews 10:14 says that Jesus Himself is our ultimate sacrifice, so the ritual commands are no longer necessary for believers to perform. In Mark 7:18-19 Jesus declared that there was no difference between clean and unclean foods.

On the other hand, the Old Testament's moral commands are still in God's plan today. The Old Testament forbids such pagan practices as fornication, adultery, homosexuality, and incest (see Leviticus 18:1-30). The Ten Commandments in Exodus 20 are also based on God's moral nature, so we are to obey them.

When we find a command or a practice in the Bible that is confusing because it reflects biblical culture, we must try to learn the principle revealed by the practice. We can often practice the principle with a change of action. It is important that we continue to obey the Bible's moral commands because they still apply today.

Day 5
Use the Bible Wisely

Today you will learn the final principle for applying the Bible to your life.

✝ Complete the four principles you have already learned for applying the Bible. The fifth principle is the one you will study today.

1. Apply the Bible according to its real _____.
2. Use the Bible as a Book of _____.
3. Use the _____ properly.
4. Use a _____ understanding.
5. Use the Bible wisely.

Sometimes the Bible writers used hyperbole, or overstatement, to make their points. In applying the Bible, recognize that some statements contain overstatement. Otherwise, some statements in the Bible would appear foolish and could not be applied meaningfully in your life.

✝ Read Matthew 5:29-30. Check all correct meanings Jesus intended by His statements.
❑ 1. Fight temptation with zeal.
❑ 2. Volunteer as an organ donor.

❑ 3. Literally tear out your eyes and cut off your hand if they lead you to sin.
❑ 4. Use mighty efforts to resist sin and evil.

Jesus urged His followers to tear out their eyes and cut off their hands rather than let these parts of the body lead them into sin. Did Jesus mean this literally? Absolutely not! He used hyperbole, or exaggeration, for effect. In Matthew 5:27-28 Jesus had warned against committing adultery by using the eyes. When He talked about removing the eyes as a source of temptation, He did not mean to cut out our eyes. He wants us to fight temptation with great zeal. Jesus wants us to use mighty efforts to resist sin and evil. He used overstatement to drive His point home. Statements 1 and 4, then, are correct.

✝ Read Matthew 5:38-41. Check all correct interpretations of Jesus' words.
❑ 1. If someone hits you, turn your head and say, "Hit me again!"
❑ 2. Don't seek revenge when you are wronged.
❑ 3. Resist the natural urge to get even.
❑ 4. If you are robbed, offer the robber all of your other possessions.

Jesus referred to the old proverb of an eye for an eye and a tooth for a tooth (see Exodus 21:24). If a blow to the mouth knocked out a tooth, the injured person would likely try to do worse than knock out an attacker's tooth. He would break a bone or inflict a fatal wound. This statement of an eye for an eye originally sought to place a limit on revenge. An injured person should do no worse to his attacker than he had received.

Jesus' words banish a spirit of revenge. The injured, toothless party is not to try to knock out his enemy's tooth. He is also to put aside any attitude of revenge by turning the other cheek.

Suppose that a robber comes to your home and knocks you down with a blow to the head. Jesus is not suggesting that you get up, turn the other side of your head, and say, "Hit me again!" He urges you to put aside a spirit of trying to get even with those who wrong you. You should have checked statements 2 and 3.

✝ Read Matthew 18:21-22. Check all of the meanings Jesus intended.
- ❑ 1. Forgive someone exactly 490 times before giving up on them.
- ❑ 2. Keep count of the number of times you forgive someone so that you can remind them.
- ❑ 3. Practice unlimited forgiveness.
- ❑ 4. Maintain a forgiving attitude.

Peter asked Jesus the extent of our forgiveness toward someone who sins against us. Peter felt that seven acts of forgiveness would be sufficient. Perhaps Peter felt that after seven acts of forgiveness, a punch in the nose would be appropriate. Jesus urged Peter to practice unlimited forgiveness. The figure of 70 times 7 symbolizes unlimited forgiveness. You don't need a computer to keep a record. Jesus calls for an unlimited extension of a forgiving attitude. Statements 3 and 4 are correct.

To apply the Bible accurately, be sure to use it wisely. That means recognizing the difference between teachings that should be taken literally and those that contain hyperbole. If overstatement is used, take time to decipher the meaning the writer or speaker intended to communicate.

✝ This week you have studied and practiced five principles for applying the Bible. Review what you have learned by filling the blanks.

1. Apply the Bible according to its real _____.

2. Use the Bible as a Book of _____.

3. Use the _____
   properly.

4. Use a _____ understanding.

5. Use the Bible _____.

✝ Write your Scripture-memory verse for this week from memory.

_____

_____

Write ways you have applied the verse this week in your life or have used it to minister to someone else.

_____

_____

Take a moment to review Ephesians 4:32, last week's Scripture-memory verse.

✝ Close your week's study with prayer. Thank God for the Bible and the direction it gives you for daily living. Commit to God the discipline required in this study and pledge to maintain a regular schedule of study during the next seven weeks.

The first two weeks of this study have laid foundational guidelines and principles for interpreting and applying the Bible. This week you will begin learning the nuts and bolts of Bible study.

What can you learn about a forest by flying over it? You can see how far the forest extends, how dense it is, and where the clearings are. What can you learn about a forest by walking through it? You can see the brooks, watch the animals, and trip over the roots. What can you learn about a forest by asking a forester? You can learn about its past, present, and future, and you can discover its place in history. Each of these views of a forest corresponds to a way to study the Bible. During the next three weeks you will study and practice three methods of Bible study.

Ways to Do Bible Study

1. Synthetic Bible study—overviewing a complete book of the Bible
2. Analytical Bible study—understanding and applying a brief Scripture passage
3. Background Bible study—exploring the history, geography, and culture of the Bible

---

This week you will learn how to use the first method—synthetic Bible study.

Day 1
Characteristics of Synthetic Bible Study

Synthetic Bible study gives you a complete overview of a book of the Bible. Synthetic Bible study presents the big picture of God's message and actions. This type of study seeks an overview of a Bible book without getting lost in a web of details.

Synthetic Bible study consists of the following distinctive ways of reading a Bible book.

1. *Read the book continuously.* This means reading the book at a single sitting. Long books such as Isaiah and Psalms may

Week 3

Ways to Do Bible Study: Synthetic Bible Study

Day 1
Characteristics of Synthetic Bible Study

Day 2
Using a Paragraph-Summary Form

Day 3
Making a Book-Summary Chart

Day 4
A Synthetic Bible Study of Philippians

Day 5
A Synthetic Bible Study of 1 Peter

SCRIPTURE-MEMORY VERSE
That I may know Him, and the power of His resurrection and the fellowship of His sufferings, being conformed to His death.
Philippians 3:10

require several hours. You can read a shorter book such as Ephesians, Philippians, or Philemon in fewer than 30 minutes. As you read the book, ignore chapter and verse divisions. Early Bible editors inserted these divisions, so they may not reflect the writer's thought pattern.

2. *Read the book independently.* Don't use a commentary or another study help during the first reading. Learn on your own with the aid of the Holy Spirit. You will be excited and surprised by what you learn!

3. *Read the book repeatedly.* You must read the book more than one time. You will need a pen and some paper or a notebook for making notes during every reading.

† Fill in the blanks to review the ways of reading that define synthetic Bible study.
1. Read the book _____.
2. Read the book _____.
3. Read the book _____.

Reading a Bible Book for Synthetic Study

1. Read the book continuously.
2. Read the book independently.
3. Read the book repeatedly.

The purposes of the first reading are to determine the main theme of the book and to learn the writer's purpose and goal. Ask yourself these questions as you read a book for the first time.

1. Who wrote the book, and to whom did he write it? Was the book written to persecuted, wavering, faithful, or confused believers?

2. What type of literature is the book? Is it poetry, prophecy, narrative, an epistle, or a combination of all of these? (See week 1, day 4 if you need to review the types of literature represented in the Bible.)

3. Why did the author write this book? Was it written to oppose sin, false teaching, or indifference? How did the

author carry out his purpose? What ideas did he present to support his purpose?

4. What arrangement of material did the writer use? Did he arrange it according to time, place, or logic?

5. What is the emotional tone of the book? Does it express joy, concern, excitement, or arguments?

Not all of these questions will apply to every book, but most of them will be useful in giving you insight into a writing's broad purpose.

If you read a book like 1 Corinthians, you can observe much in the first reading. You can learn that the church was filled with people who were proud and ready to argue. They were practicing sexual immorality. They allowed false teaching. They practiced sensational spiritual gifts such as speaking in tongues and working miracles while failing to love one another. They had not given generously. Many times Paul used the phrase *now* or *now concerning* (see 1 Corinthians 7:1; 8:1; 11:2; 12:1; 16:1) to introduce a new topic for discussion.

If you read the Book of Romans or Ephesians, you will see a change of emphasis between Romans 11 and 12 and between Ephesians 3 and 4. In both books Paul spent the first chapters outlining important theological truths. In the later chapters he applied these truths in his readers' lives. Both books contain the words *now* or *therefore* (see Romans 12:1; Ephesians 4:1), showing that Paul is changing from one topic to another.

✝ **Read Luke 1:1-4. State Luke's purpose in writing the Book of Luke.**

_____

_____

_____

Although these verses are not an entire book of the Bible, they give you an idea of what the entire book is about. Luke stated that he wrote the book to provide an accurate chronological account of events in Jesus' life so that his readers would know the truth.

✝ Now read the Book of Philemon at one sitting. Without using any Bible-study aids, answer the five key questions introduced in this session.

1. Who wrote the book, and to whom did he write it?

_____

_____

2. What type of literature is the book?

_____

3. Why did the author write this book? How did the author carry out his purpose? What ideas did he present to support his purpose?

_____

_____

_____

4. What arrangement of material did the writer use? Did he arrange it according to time, place, or logic?

_____

5. What is the emotional tone of the book? Does it express joy, concern, excitement, or arguments?

_____

Even one reading of Philemon reveals Paul's purpose and circumstances when he wrote this epistle. I'm sure you were able to record the other information about the book, as well. Tomorrow you will go deeper in your study of Philemon.

✝ This week's Scripture-memory verse is Philippians 3:10. Begin memorizing it today, using the Scripture-memory card at the center of your workbook.

Day 2
Using a Paragraph-Summary Form

In day 1 you learned to read the Bible continuously and independently at one sitting. You know that a continuous reading of a book of the Bible gives you a sweeping picture of what the book contains. You learned to look for the book's purpose, content, and structure on your first reading, without consulting Bible-study aids. Today you will focus on the third characteristic of reading for synthetic Bible study.

✝ Can you recall the third distinctive way you read a book of the Bible for synthetic study? Write it below.

In addition to reading a book of the Bible continuously and independently, you need to read it repeatedly. Today you will observe the way additional readings help uncover the book's hidden treasures of meaning.

As you repeatedly read a book of the Bible, read from different translations. Such contemporary versions as the *New King James*, the *New International Version*, the *Good News Bible*, the *New American Standard Bible*, and the *Holman Christian Standard Bible* illuminate different ideas. *The Amplified Bible* may help you learn the meanings of words, although it is difficult to read quickly because the text includes many synonyms. Be aware that some Bibles are paraphrases. Although a paraphrase is not the same as a translation, many Bible students find a paraphrase helpful for comparing with another translation or for clarifying difficult language.

As you read a book for the second time, build on what you observed in your first reading.

- Observe more about the author's purpose and how he expressed it.
- Discover more about the writer's time, place, and circumstances.
- Notice words or phrases that frequently appear.
- Look for changes of mood or shifts in location.
- Notice a change in the topic of discussion.
- Rely on such connective words as *therefore, because, so that,* and *since.*
- Make a determined effort to improve your grasp of the facts about the book.

Add what you observe to the notes you made during your first reading.

In the second reading of a book, observe the paragraph divisions. Remember that these were later added and were not part of God's original revelation. They represent God guiding Bible editors to format a book by logical divisions. They are useful as a means of dividing the writer's thoughts into sections.

☦ **Look at Romans 12. What function do the paragraph divisions seem to serve?**

This passage is part of a teaching letter by Paul. The divisions of each paragraph are made on the basis of different topics discussed.

☦ **Now look at Genesis 12. What do the paragraph divisions indicate in this passage?**

This is in a narrative section of Genesis. The divisions of each paragraph show different geographical locations.

You will find that in most types of biblical writing, most paragraph divisions help indicate a summary of the writer's thoughts. The paragraph divisions of Revelation, for example, often show features of the visions the Lord Jesus gave to John. However, the paragraph divisions of the Old Testament books of poetry, such as Psalms or Proverbs, are not useful for study. The editors indented each verse as a separate paragraph.

A paragraph-summary form can be used to prepare a summary of each paragraph you identify in your reading. Examine the form below. Follow these steps to use the form.

1. Duplicate or manually copy the form to use with each paragraph in your reading.
2. Record the Bible reference that composes the paragraph.
3. Use a sentence(s) or phrase(s) to summarize the content.
4. Look for connections between paragraphs.
5. Think of a title or theme to summarize the content.

Paragraph Summary

Paragraph location: _____

Summary: _____

_____

_____

Connections with other paragraphs: _____

_____

_____

Summarizing title or theme: _____

_____

_____

• M A S T E R   C O P Y   •   D U P L I C A T E   B E F O R E   U S I N G •

> ## Using a Paragraph-Summary Form
>
> 1. Make a copy of the form for each paragraph.
> 2. Record the Bible reference that composes the paragraph.
> 3. Summarize the paragraph's content.
> 4. Look for connections between the paragraphs.
> 5. Think of a title or theme to summarize the content.

✝ **Read Philemon again, this time noting, studying, and analyzing each paragraph. Identify the paragraphs in the version you are reading. Duplicate or manually copy the form "Paragraph Summary" on page 59 to prepare a summary of each paragraph you identify.**

How did you do? Tomorrow you will learn how to put your paragraph summaries together to get an overview of the entire Bible book you are studying.

Day 3
Making a Book-Summary Chart

This week you are learning how to do synthetic Bible study, which gives you a broad overview of a book of the Bible.

✝ **Recall the three characteristics of reading when you do synthetic Bible study.**
1. Read the book _____.
2. Read the book _____.
3. Read the book _____.

Look back to day 1 if you weren't able to recall the distinctive ways you are learning to read for synthetic Bible study. Because one of those characteristics is reading a book repeatedly, yesterday you read the Book of Philemon for the second time. How many times should you read a book of the Bible? That depends on the book's length, your grasp of the material, and the amount of time you have. Each reading should give more insight into the book. Each time you read, you will want to add observations to the notes you have made about purpose, content, and structure. You will have further impressions about the content of paragraphs while you are reading.

At some point in your reading you will want to summarize what you have learned about the content of the book. You can use a book-summary chart for this purpose.

A book-summary chart is a visual sketch that outlines the book's content. Using a book-summary chart, like the one shown on page 62, has three major advantages.

1. The chart helps you summarize the key ideas found in a book of the Bible.

2. The chart helps you see the relationship between paragraphs in a chapter or section of a book.

3. The chart becomes a useful memory device to help you learn chapter and book content.

To complete a book-summary chart, use a Bible with paragraph divisions. Here are the steps to follow.

1. *Identify the chapters or major divisions in the book.* List these in the left column of the book-summary chart. In some cases, a major division of a book might include material that is found in more than one chapter. Remember, editors placed chapter and verse divisions in your Bible to help in Bible study. They are not part of the original text. If you need to include material from more than one chapter when listing a major division, feel free to do so.

2. *Write a title for each chapter or major division.* In the next column on the book-summary chart, write the title you would give to the material in each chapter or major division.

3. *Summarize each paragraph in the chapters or major divisions.* Following the process you learned yesterday, write a brief summary of each paragraph in the chapters or major divisions. Write your summaries in the third column of the book-summary chart.

4. *Write on another sheet of paper an outline of the Bible book.* Base your outline on the major divisions you identified. These major divisions may reflect different times, places, or ideas. Beneath these major divisions you will place small

Book Summary

Book of the Bible:_____

Chapter or Major Division	Title or Theme of Chapter or Major Division	Summary or Key Ideas of Paragraphs in Chapter or Major Division

divisions. These divisions may consist of chapters, individual paragraphs, or groups of paragraphs. You can learn by comparing your outline with another outline in a commentary or an introduction to a book of the Bible. Your outline does not need to match exactly. However, carefully notice whether your outline greatly differs from what you find in other reference works.

Prepare your book-summary chart and your outline independently. Don't seek help until you are ready to check your work. You will find great excitement in using God's help to discover what the Bible teaches. If you begin your study by relying too much on reference works, you will not develop your own creative style, and you may miss what God wants to teach you personally.

Using a Book-Summary Chart

1. Identify the chapters or major divisions.
2. Write a title for each chapter or major division.
3. Summarize each paragraph in the chapters or major divisions.
4. Write an outline of the book.

✝ Read Philemon again. This time follow the steps you have read to complete the "Book Summary" on page 62. Make a copy of the form to use with this exercise.

By now you should have memorized this week's Scripture-memory verse. Write it here for practice, being sure to include the reference.

_____

_____

_____

_____

Day 4
A Synthetic Bible Study of Philippians

So far this week you have become acquainted with synthetic Bible study as a method to take a broad look at a book of the Bible. You have learned that this method requires reading the Bible book continuously, independently, and repeatedly.

Today you will use what you have learned to complete a synthetic Bible study of Philippians. Your lessons today and tomorrow will be long, but they will provide the important practice needed to master synthetic Bible study.

† Read the Book of Philippians independently at a single sitting. As you read the book, make your own observations by answering the questions you used in day 1.

1. Who wrote Philippians, and to whom did he write it?

_____

_____

_____

2. What type of literature is the book?

_____

3. Why did Paul write this book? How did he carry out his purpose? What ideas did he present to support his purpose?

_____

_____

_____

4. What arrangement of material did Paul use? Did he arrange it according to time, place, or logic?

_____

5. What is the emotional tone of the book? Does it express joy, concern, excitement, or arguments?

_____

You might have made some of the following observations in your first reading.

1. Philippians was written by Paul while he was in prison, probably in Rome. His comments in 1:13-14 suggest imprisonment, and his reference to "those of Caesar's household" in 4:22 points toward Rome. Paul wrote the book to the church at Philippi, a group of Christian friends who had been considerate to him (4:14-16). Some strife was present in the church (1:15; 2:1-4; 4:2), and false teachers were unsettling the Christians (3:2-6,17-21).

2. Philippians is a teaching letter.

3. Paul wrote the letter to inform the church about his personal situation (1:12-14). He also wanted to encourage them to steadfast Christian living (1:27-28), to urge them to avoid strife (2:3-4), to introduce Timothy (2:19-24), to explain the plight of Epaphroditus (2:25-30), and to warn against false teachers (3:2-6). He specifically rebuked two women in the church (4:2-3) who were apparently quarreling.

4. The book is arranged by logic.

5. Paul shows several different moods throughout the book. In 1:3 he displays a thankful spirit. In 1:12-14 he shows a cheerful, accepting attitude despite his imprisonment. In 3:2-6 he shows passion and excitement as he opposes false teachers. In 3:12-14 he demonstrates spiritual intensity in his commitment to Christ. An outlook of joy appears in 4:4.

✝ Read Philippians again. This time try to summarize the paragraph content, using a copy of the form "Paragraph Summary" on page 59 for each paragraph.

If you used the paragraph divisions of the *New American Standard Bible,* you may have made the following summaries of the paragraphs in chapter 1.

- Verses 1-2: Paul greets the Philippians.
- Verses 3-11: Paul thanks God for the spiritual progress of the Philippians, declares his love for them, and prays that their love will grow.
- Verses 12-26: Paul explains the results of his imprisonment and rejoices that some are preaching Christ. He believes that God will let him live in order to encourage them to live for Christ.
- Verses 27-30: Paul urges them to endure persecution without being frightened.

✝ **You are almost ready to complete a book-summary chart on Philippians. But first answer the following questions as a way of identifying the major divisions of the book.**

What is Paul doing in 1:1-2?

_____

What is Paul's activity in 1:3-11?

_____

What subject is Paul discussing in 1:12-26?

_____

What are the Philippians' spiritual needs that Paul discusses in 1:27—2:18?

_____

Whom does Paul commend in 2:19-30?

_____

In what areas does Paul give a warning in 3:1—4:1?

_____

What specific problems does Paul mention in 4:2-9?

_____

How does Paul conclude his letter in 4:10-23?

_____

Now complete a book-summary chart for Philippians, using the chart on page 68. Indicate the major divisions of Philippians on your chart. Also include the chapter titles or themes and summaries of key ideas. On a separate sheet of paper write an outline of the book.

Did you find it difficult to do a synthetic study of a whole book of the Bible? Maybe you are not accustomed to viewing an entire Bible book as a whole. When you gain more practice, you will find it valuable to be able to quickly grasp the major purpose, theme, and ideas in a Bible book. Tomorrow you will complete another synthetic Bible study to become more comfortable with this method.

Book Summary

Book of the Bible:_____

Chapter or Major Division	Title or Theme of Chapter or Major Division	Summary or Key Ideas of Paragraphs in Chapter or Major Division

Day 5

A Synthetic Bible Study of 1 Peter

Today you will complete another synthetic Bible study to practice this new Bible-study skill.

✝ Read 1 Peter at a single sitting without the help of study aids. Make notes by answering the following questions.

1. Who wrote 1 Peter, and to whom did he write it?

_____

_____

2. What type of literature is the book?

_____

3. Why did Peter write this book? How did he carry out his purpose? What ideas did he present to support his purpose?

_____

_____

_____

4. What arrangement of material did Peter use? Did he arrange it according to time, place, or logic?

_____

5. What is the emotional tone of the book? Does it express joy, concern, excitement, or arguments?

_____

Here are our observations about 1 Peter. Compare them with the observations you made during your first reading.

1. Peter probably wrote the letter from Rome. His reference to Babylon in 5:13 is probably a way of describing Rome. New Testament Rome was as wicked as ancient Babylon. The readers of 1 Peter lived in the provinces of Pontus, Galatia, Cappadocia, Asia, and Bithynia. In New Testament times this was the northern part of Asia Minor.

2. First Peter is a teaching letter.

3. Peter wrote this book to a group of Christians who were facing painful suffering. The topic of suffering appears in every chapter of the book in such passages as 1:6-9; 2:18-25; 3:13-22; 4:12-19; and 5:10-11. The presence of so many references to suffering indicates that this is the major theme of the book.

4. The subject matter proceeds logically. In the middle chapters of the book Peter placed some material that shows a Christian response in different situations. In 2:13-17 Peter talks about the Christian and government. In 2:18-25 he discusses slaves and their masters. In 3:1-7 Peter discusses the Christian home. In 3:8-12 he discusses Christians' relationships with one another.

5. Peter demonstrates varied moods throughout 1 Peter. In 1:3-4 he expresses praise to God. In 1:13; 2:1,13,18; 3:1; and many other passages he shows earnestness. His earnestness is also mixed with much compassion in 4:12 and with pastoral encouragement in 5:1-4.

✝ Now complete paragraph summaries for 1 Peter, using copies of the form "Paragraph Summary" on page 59.

Here is a sample of paragraph summaries from 1 Peter 1, using paragraph divisions in the *New American Standard Bible*.

- Verses 1-2: Peter greets his readers.
- Verses 3-12: Peter praises God for his living hope and shows that the Holy Spirit revealed the plan of salvation to the Old Testament prophets.
- Verses 13-21: Peter calls his readers to disciplined, holy living because of the high cost of their salvation.

- Verses 22-25: Peter urges his readers to express their new life with brotherly love for one another.

Are you satisfied with your paragraph summaries? Remember, your paragraph summaries do not have to be exactly like anyone else's to be correct. However, it is important that you are satisfied that you have done a good job with the summaries before you go on to the next step, which is to make a book-summary chart.

✝ Before making your book-summary chart, answer these questions to identify the major divisions of 1 Peter.

Who performs the work mentioned in 1:1-2?

_____

For what is Peter thankful in 1:3-5?

_____

What is the effect of the trials in 1:6-9?

_____

What character trait is Peter demanding from his readers in 1:13—2:3?

_____

Why is he demanding this trait?

_____

How are the readers to show this trait?

_____

What group is being described in 2:4-10?

_____

How are they to reflect their position?

_____

List the subjects Peter is treating in 2:11—3:12.

_____

_____

What groups would find these subjects a challenge?

_____

Who would be encouraged by the commands and promises in 3:13—4:19?

_____

What situation would these readers be facing?

_____

What group is addressed in Peter's final chapter?

_____

What encouragement does Peter give to their obedience?

_____

Now complete a book-summary chart for 1 Peter, using the chart on page 73. Indicate the major divisions of the book on your chart. Also include the chapter titles or themes and summaries of key ideas. Then on a separate sheet of paper write an outline of the book.

Book Summary

Book of the Bible:_____

Chapter or Major Division	Title or Theme of Chapter or Major Division	Summary or Key Ideas of Paragraphs in Chapter or Major Division

We hope you are becoming comfortable with synthetic Bible study as a result of your work this week and will find this method useful in the future. Next week you will study another way to approach the study of God's Word.

† Write this week's Scripture-memory verse from memory.

_____

_____

_____

_____

As you memorized this verse this week, what new meanings did the Holy Spirit reveal to you?

_____

_____

_____

_____

Take a moment to review the previous weeks' Scripture-memory verses.

† Close your study this week in prayer thanking God for Paul, Peter, and others who were obedient to Him in recording for us God's transforming Word.

This week you will learn another way to do Bible study. Last week you studied synthetic Bible study, which gives you a broad, sweeping picture of a book of the Bible. Synthetic Bible study is a good method to use in beginning the study of a book.

You may not teach or study whole books of the Bible at one time. Most often you will work with one small section or passage. The kind of study that can help you with a small passage is called analytical Bible study. Analytical Bible study gives you a detailed view of a Bible book. Here the words, sentences, and paragraphs become important. The prayers, commands, and promises of Scripture have new meaning. We get this view of the Bible by slow, deliberate study with close observation. This Bible-study method makes the details of a Bible passage become clear.

Analytical Bible study consists of five elements, which are illustrated in the analytical Bible-study arch.

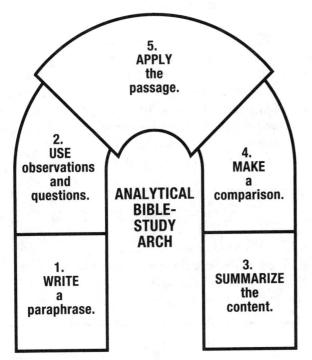

Each day you will study and practice using one of these elements. At the end of the week you should be able to draw the arch and label the elements.

Week 4

Ways to Do Bible Study: Analytical Bible Study

Day 1
Writing a Paraphrase

Day 2
Using Observations and Questions

Day 3
Summarizing the Content

Day 4
Making a Comparison

Day 5
Applying the Passage

SCRIPTURE-MEMORY VERSE
Be anxious for nothing, but in everything by prayer and supplication with thanksgiving let your requests be made known to God. And the peace of God, which surpasses all comprehension, shall guard your hearts and your minds in Christ Jesus.
Philippians 4:6-7

Day 1
Writing a Paraphrase

There are four steps in paraphrasing a Scripture passage.

1. *Select a section for analysis.* If you are going to study, teach, or speak on a Scripture passage, it is best to use a paragraph of Scripture, since a paragraph is the basic unit of thought.

2. *Read the section several times in different Bible versions.* As you read the paragraph, notice the main verbs used in the sentences. Observe whether they indicate statements, exclamations, questions, or commands. Observe important nouns in the sentences and what they mean. Carefully note any words or phrases that modify the nouns. The modifiers provide information you can use in a paraphrase.

3. *Write the section in your own words.* Don't copy the words of a modern translation or a paraphrase. Express the biblical writer's thoughts, attitudes, and purposes as you understand them. Use modern English words. You may use several words to say what a biblical writer has said in a few words. Be careful to maintain the meaning of the verses.

4. *Check your paraphrase against a modern translation.* You may learn that your paraphrase has brought out a different idea from the translation you have consulted. If this is true, you may have given the verse the wrong meaning. Revise your paraphrase after checking it with other translations.

Writing a Paraphrase

1. Select a section for analysis.
2. Read the section several times in different Bible versions.
3. Write the section in your own words.
4. Check your paraphrase against a modern translation.

✝ **Read Philippians 4:4-7. Make a copy of "Analytical Bible Study" on page 77. Follow the steps to write a paraphrase of these verses in the column "Paraphrase."**

Analytical Bible Study

Paraphrase	Observations and Questions	Summary	Comparison	Application

Here are some problems we identified in paraphrasing Philippians 4:4-7. Check to see whether your paraphrase addressed these concerns.

- The verbs in verses 4-7 are commands except for the promise in verse 7. Obeying the command in verse 6 is a prerequisite to experiencing the promise in verse 7.
- The *King James Version* uses the word *moderation* in verse 5. Can you find a word that expresses the thought more accurately?
- Can you find three words for *prayer* in verse 6?
- How would you define God's *peace* as it is used in verse 7?
- What did Paul mean by *heart* and *mind* in verse 7?

The purpose of writing a paraphrase is to help you understand what the author is saying. A paraphrase is the best way to discover the biblical writer's ideas and thoughts. As the beginning point for analytical Bible study, a paraphrase will help you complete the other parts of analytical study more accurately.

✝ **Your Scripture-memory assignment this week is Philippians 4:6-7, a part of the passage you have paraphrased. Begin memorizing these verses, using the Scripture-memory card at the center of your workbook.**

Day 2
Using Observations and Questions

Yesterday you examined and practiced the first element in analytical Bible study.

✝ **Supply the first element on the analytical Bible-study arch at the top of the next page.**

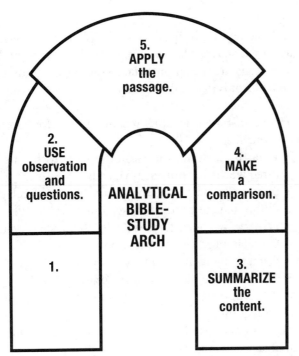

Yesterday you learned how to paraphrase a passage, and you practiced paraphrasing Philippians 4:4-7. Now you are ready to make observations and ask questions about the passage.

One way to analyze a Bible passage more deeply is to ask questions. For example, you might ask, "Who?" Who wrote this material? Who are the characters involved? For whom is the passage intended?

Or you might ask the question "What?" What is happening in the text? What does it say to us?

"Why?" is another good question. Why did the writer say these things, and in what context were they written?

"So what?" may be the most important question of all. What difference does this passage make to people today?

Asking questions about the passage stimulates your thinking and forces you to take the Bible seriously. This will help you apply its teachings more completely to your life.

†Read again Philippians 4:4-7. What questions would you ask to discover the meanings of these verses? Write your questions in the appropriate column on your copy of the chart "Analytical Bible Study."

Here are some questions we identified. How do they compare with your list?

- What Bible-study tool would give you the meanings of the three words for *prayer* in verse 6?
- In verse 6 what practical activity does Paul challenge the Philippians to perform instead of worry?
- Why do we need to present the requests of verse 6 to God? Does He need the information?
- What is the relationship between verses 6 and 7? How would you learn the meaning of *the peace of God*?
- What does the word *guard* in verse 7 suggest about God's protection?

You can also use observations to analyze a Bible passage. You can observe details like the following.

- *Key words*. What do the verbs, nouns, adjectives, or adverbs mean?
- *The type of statement*. Is it offering advice, warning, exclamation, or promise?
- *Contrasts or comparisons*. What is the writer comparing or contrasting?
- *Repetition*. Are words or phrases repeated?
- *Questions*. Often a question in a passage introduces new ideas or summaries.
- *Connectives*. Look for words such as *but, if, therefore,* or *in order that*. What do they suggest about the meaning of the passage?
- *Grammar*. Look at verb tenses and the use of pronouns, adjectives, and adverbs.
- *Atmosphere*. What is the general tone of the passage?
- *Literary form*. Is it poetry, prophecy, narrative, an epistle, or a parable?
- *General structure*. How are the ideas in the passage related to one another?

✝ **What observations would be important to explore in Philippians 4:4-7? Add these to the second column of your copy of the chart "Analytical Bible Study."**

I'm sure you recorded the need to explore the meanings of key words in the passage, Paul's imperative statements and promises, the contrast evident in verse 6, the repetition of key ideas, and the confident and deeply spiritual tone. You may have noted other details, as well.

Often your observations will lead you to more questions rather than to answers. These questions will be of two basic types.
1. You will ask questions about the meanings of certain terms, places, or statements in the Bible.
2. You will ask questions about the meaning, significance, and application to life of what is in the Bible.

List your questions along with your observations. Here are some ways to answer your questions about a passage.
- Use a dictionary to define unfamiliar words.
- Read different translations to obtain the meaning of a phrase or a puzzling statement.
- Study other biblical passages that are cross-referenced in your study Bible.
- Think, study, meditate, and pray.
- Use a Bible-study aid such as a book on Bible culture, history, or social life.
- Use a commentary on a passage only after you have struggled to arrive at your own answer.

✝ **Use one of these suggestions to explore a question or an observation you made today about Philippians 4:4-7. Write what you learn. Use the margin if needed.**

_____

_____

_____

Day 3
Summarizing the Content

This week you are studying the second way to do Bible study, analytical Bible study. You have already learned and practiced two of five elements that compose this type of Bible study.

✝ On the analytical Bible-study arch below, record the two components of analytical study you have learned so far.

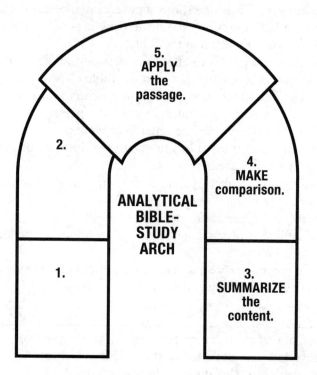

5.
APPLY
the
passage.

2.

4.
MAKE
comparison.

ANALYTICAL
BIBLE-
STUDY
ARCH

1.

3.
SUMMARIZE
the
content.

After you have paraphrased, made observations, and asked questions about a Scripture passage, you are ready to take your study a step further. Next it is helpful to write a summary of what you have learned about the Scripture passage, based on the paraphrase, observations, and questions you have recorded. A summary helps you articulate and clarify what you have learned about the Scripture passage.

You can use two methods to summarize a passage. First, you can use the observations and questions you have recorded about the passage to state conclusions about the passage's meaning. Your summary states what you have learned about the passage, what you believe the biblical writer meant, and how the passage may be used. Make sure that your summary encompasses everything in the passage and conveys the feeling as well as the message of the content.

✝ Try composing your own summary of Philippians 4:4-7. Write it under "Summary" on your copy of the chart "Analytical Bible Study."

Your summary may have included some of the following ideas. Paul emphatically commanded the Philippians to rejoice. Their joy was to be in the Lord, and it was to be unchanging, in spite of circumstances like the one Paul found himself in. He also told them to be forbearing or gentle. A gentle person does not insist on his rights but respects others' integrity. This person's fairness and sense of purpose attracts others to Christ. In verse 6 Paul was not content merely to tell the Philippians not to worry. He gave them a practical activity to perform instead of worrying. They were to tell God their requests. We do not tell God our requests in order to inform Him. He already knows about our needs. We want to relieve ourselves of the anxiety they cause. Through prayer we transfer the responsibility to Him, and we center our lives in Him by praying with thanksgiving. The peace of God mentioned in verse 7 is much more than happy feelings and a carefree lifestyle. The word refers to the wholeness or balance God gives to someone who fears and follows Him. The word *guard* in verse 7 is a military word. It is used outside the Bible to describe a Roman sentry in the act of guarding something. The heart and the mind in verse 7 make up our entire personality. God will keep watch over our mind, our emotions, and our will.

In addition to making summarizing conclusions about a passage, it is helpful to construct an outline of the passage. The purpose of this outline is to describe the content of the biblical passage—to state your understanding of what the biblical writer is saying. To make this outline, use the declarations, commands, or questions of a paragraph as the main points. The modifiers of these main verbs will become the smaller subheads beneath the major points. Use as few words as possible and try to use words that allow you to visualize the content of the passage. When possible, use words that come directly from the text itself.

Your outline does not need to have rhyming words or other special features to catch a listener's attention. Sometimes a teacher may use repeated or rhyming words to make a passage vivid and memorable. This may be helpful if it is natural, but you should not force a passage into an artificial outline.

Prepare this outline without outside help for the content. After you have made your outline, give the passage a title.

✝ Write an outline of Philippians 4:4-7 in the third column of your copy of the chart along with the summary you have written. Your outline and your summary should bring together all you have learned about the passage to this point.

Writing a summary and outline are important steps because they lay the groundwork for applying the Bible passage to your life or to someone else's life.

✝ By now you should have memorized Philippians 4:6-7. Write the verses from memory.

_____

_____

_____

_____

_____

Day 4
Making a Comparison

Today you will learn the fourth element in analytical Bible study. First review what you have studied this week.

✝ On the analytical Bible-study arch on this page, label the three elements in analytical Bible study that you have studied this week.

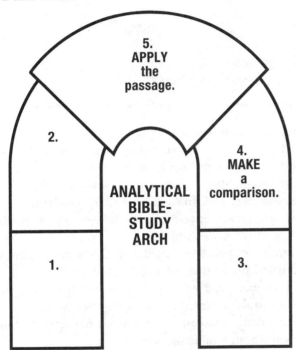

After you have determined the meaning of a Bible passage, it is helpful to compare the passage with other passages that teach or illustrate the same message. This type of study is called comparative Bible study. As you learn how to do this type of study during this session, you will need the following Bible-study resources: a study or reference Bible, a concordance, a topical Bible, a New Testament introduction, and a commentary on Philippians.

When you are doing a comparative study of a given passage, you make four comparisons:

1. Use topics or subjects to compare.
2. Use words to compare.
3. Use persons or events to compare.
4. Use the context to compare.

Let's take a close look at these and learn how we can use each comparison to gain a better understanding of Philippians 4:4-7.

Making a Comparison

1. Use topics or subjects to compare.
2. Use words to compare.
3. Use persons or events to compare.
4. Use the context to compare.

Use topics or subjects to compare. Ask, What is the subject or topic of this passage I am studying, and what does this passage say about it? Then compare what other passages in the Bible say about the same subject. You can use several ways to find other passages that deal with the subject you are studying.

- Most good study or reference Bibles refer you to passages that deal with the same subject.
- A number of passages that deal with the subject are gathered and listed under that subject in a topical Bible.
- Your memory is a valuable resource because you will recall having studied related passages at other times.
- Occasionally, you can locate related passages by looking up the subject in a Bible dictionary.

If you are studying a passage that deals with an incident in the life of Christ, compare what the other Gospel accounts say about the same incident. One Gospel may give a detail about Jesus' deeds and words that another Gospel omits. This will give you a more complete understanding of what Jesus said and did.

The New Testament passage may quote an Old Testament passage or refer to an incident in the Old Testament. A comparative study of the Old Testament text can help you better understand why the New Testament author referred to the Old Testament.

✝ Read Philippians 4:4-7. What would you identify as the general subject this passage deals with?

_____

_____

This passage addresses worry and anxiety or the need for prayer and thanksgiving.

✝ Compare other passages that deal with the same subject. Using other resources, find and compare other passages. List some of the passages you discovered that deal with the same subject.

_____

_____

_____

Use words to compare. The resources we have listed will help you compare words. But a concordance is probably the best resource for finding other passages that have the same words as the passage you are studying. A concordance is particularly helpful for comparing often-used words like *prayer, joy, anger, Holy Spirit,* and so on.

✝ Take the word *supplication* in Philippians 4:6 and compare the way the word is used in other Bible passages. Use the excerpt on page 88 from a concordance to get started.[1] Then use other resources that are available to you. What meanings do the other passages add to the use of this word in Philippians 4:6?

_____

_____

SUNK Ps. 38:2, Thine arrows have **s** deep

SUNRISE Luke 1:78, the **S** from on high shall visit us

SUNSHINE 2 Sam. 23:4, Through **s** after rain

SUPERIORITY 1 Cor. 2:1, not come with **s** of speech

SUPPER John 13:4, rose from **s** and laid aside
1 Cor. 11:20, not to eat the Lord's **S**
Rev. 19:9, marriage **s** of the Lamb

SUPPLANTS Prov. 30:23, maidservant ...**s** her mistress

SUPPLICATION Ex. 9:28, Make **s** to the Lord
Ps. 28:2, Hear the voice of my **s-s**
Dan. 9:3, seek Him by prayer and **s-s**

SUPPLY Is. 3:1, s of bread ... s of water

SUPPORT Matt. 10:10, worker is worthy of his **s**
Ex. 17:12; 2 Tim 4:16

SURE—trust Num. 32:23, be **s** your sin will find you out
Ps. 19:7, testimony of the Lord is s
Heb. 13:18, s that we have a good conscience
2 Pet. 1:19, prophetic word made more **s**

SURELY Gen. 2:17, eat from it you shall **s** die
Gen. 28:16, **S** the Lord is in this place
Deut. 14:22, **s** tithe all the produce
Ps. 23:6, **S** goodness and lovingkindness
Is. 53:4, **S** our griefs He ... bore
Mark 14:70, **S** you are one of them
Heb. 6:14, **s** BLESS YOU ... **S** MULTIPLY YOU
Ex. 31:13; 2 Sam. 17:11; Job 35:13; Jer. 23:39

SURFACE Gen. 1:2; 7:18; Job 38:30

SURMISE Acts 27:27, sailors began to **s**

SURPASS 2 Chr. 9:6. You **s** the report I heard
Eph. 1:19, the **s-ing** greatness of His power 2:7, the **s-ing** riches of His grace

Here is a helpful hint for comparing words or topics. In addition to looking up the word or topic you are studying, also look up synonyms (words or topics that mean the same) and antonyms (words or topics that are the opposite).

Use persons or events to compare. Often your study will reveal persons or events in the Bible that illustrate the importance of practicing a truth you are studying. At other times you will discover a passage that highlights a person who ignored the truth you are studying. This kind of comparison helps you realize the way those concepts have worked out in human experience.

---

†Name someone in the Bible or a biblical event that illustrates one of the concepts in Philippians 4:4-7.

_____

Use a concordance or a Bible dictionary to read about that person or event in the Bible. What insight did you gain that illuminates the meaning of the Philippians passage? Write a brief description of what you discovered.

_____

_____

_____

_____

Use the context to compare. When you do a comparative study of the Bible, be careful to observe the context of the passage. If you ignore the context, you may make a serious error in the interpretation of the passage. Sometimes people will pull a passage out of context to make it say what they want it to say and not allow the passage to communicate God's message. This is referred to as proof-texting a passage. A good study or reference Bible, a concordance, or a New Testament and Old Testament introduction can give you the proper context of the passage you are studying.

✝ Use a resource to discover the context in which Paul wrote Philippians. Write a brief description of what you learned.

_____

_____

_____

_____

Reinforce the comparative study you did today by making notes in the column "Comparison" on your copy of the chart "Analytical Bible Study."

Remember the importance of beginning to add to your personal library of Bible-study resources. By this point in your study you are realizing that need more and more. In future weeks you will come to believe even more firmly in the importance of having Bible-study resources at your disposal. Review page 14 in the introduction to this study. Consider the resources recommended and others you may have discovered during your study. Establish a plan by which you can build your library of Bible-study resources.

---

[1] *Master Study Bible*, New American Standard Version (Nashville: Holman Bible Publishers, 1981), 2347.

Day 5
Applying the Passage

This week you are learning how to do analytical Bible study, and you have learned four of the five components of this in-depth method of study.

✝ On the Bible-study arch below, name the four elements you have studied to this point.

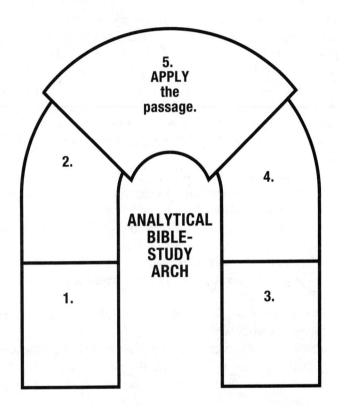

5.
APPLY
the
passage.

2.

4.

ANALYTICAL
BIBLE-
STUDY
ARCH

1.

3.

Notice the fifth element, which you will study today. You have learned how to discover a passage's meaning by writing a paraphrase, using observations and questions, summarizing the content, and making a comparison. Everything you have done this week has brought you to the point of applying a Scripture passage to your needs or to the needs of others.

Your application of a Scripture passage must be based on the meaning of the passage. As you learned in week 2, sometimes a passage of Scripture will give you a principle you can apply to your life. Sometimes your application of that principle will result in a different action from the one mentioned in the Bible. For example, you will recall that an equivalent of a "holy kiss" (2 Corinthians 13:12) is a handshake.

Be very careful when you apply biblical principles to your life. Do you remember our discussion about eating meat offered to idols? (See page 39 in week 2, day 2.) Paul decided to give up eating such meat if it offended another Christian. However, we should not give up all practices merely because they might offend others. Some Christians might feel that they should not share the gospel for fear of offending someone. The Bible clearly conveys the expectation that every believer share the gospel. The principle is not that we should give up a practice just because we offend another person with it. The principle is that we should give up any unnecessary practice if it harms another Christian. Careful and thoughtful use of the Bible can prevent errors in applying its teachings.

If you apply the Bible to others' needs or to your church, be careful not to apply the Bible to others without first using it on yourself. Also, be cautious in announcing to others that you have applied the Bible to them. Much prayer should precede any effort to apply the Bible to someone else's life.

When you apply the Bible to yourself, make your application—

- *personal.* Write an application for yourself in a sentence with *I, me,* or *my* in it.
- *practical.* It must be something you can do, not something beyond possibility.
- *specific.* If God has convicted you about prayerlessness, your application must include a specific plan to begin to pray.

Use probing questions like the following when applying the Bible to yourself.

- *What am I to believe?* Is something in the passage about God, Jesus Christ, the Holy Spirit, grace, mercy, forgiveness, hope, or eternal life?
- *What am I to do?* Do I need to change some actions or confess some sins? Do I need to put away attitudes like fear, worry, hate, resentment, or jealousy?
- *What have I learned about relationships?* Does this passage teach me a new truth about my relationship with God through Jesus Christ? Do I see new insights into my relationships with others in my family, community, congregation, or world?
- *Is there a promise I need to claim?* Are there conditions for claiming this promise? Is there a word of encouragement or hope for me?

Don't use this list of questions in a mechanical way but to search for ways to apply a Scripture passage. Try to find a command, promise, or example by which you can apply God's grace to your life.

✝ Use the previous questions to apply Philippians 4:4-7 to your life.

What am I to believe?

_____

_____

What am I to do?

_____

_____

What have I learned about relationships?

_____

_____

Is there a promise I need to claim?

_____

_____

Now write your applications in the final column of your copy of the chart "Analytical Bible Study." Remember, these applications should be personal, practical, and specific.

Applying the Bible to Yourself

- What am I to believe?
- What am I to do?
- What have I learned about relationships?
- Is there a promise I need to claim?

This brings you to the end of your study of analytical Bible study. We hope you have mastered the five components of analytical study. These methods are valuable tools for helping you dig beneath the surface of a passage to discover the rich truths God has for you.

† Review your week's study by labeling the sections of the Bible-study arch below.

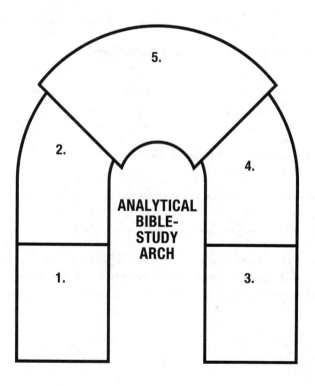

ANALYTICAL BIBLE-STUDY ARCH

5.

2.

4.

1.

3.

✝ You have applied this week's Scripture-memory verse to your life as part of today's study. Think about someone you know who could benefit from the message of these verses. Share the verses with that person from memory, either as a ministry or as a way to introduce the person to the peace God offers through a relationship with Jesus Christ. Close in prayer asking God to guide you as you share these verses with another person.

Week 5

Ways to Do Bible Study: Background Bible Study

Day 1
What to Look For

Day 2
The Historical Background

Day 3
The Geographical Background

Day 4
The Cultural Background

Day 5
The Sociological Background

Scripture-Memory Verse
Whoever drinks of the water that I shall give him shall never thirst; but the water that I shall give him shall become in him a well of water springing up to eternal life.

John 4:14

This week you will study a third way to do Bible study. In week 3 you learned how to do synthetic Bible study, which gives you a broad overview of a book of the Bible. Last week you learned to analyze a specific Bible passage to understand and apply its meaning. This approach is called analytical Bible study.

In addition to these methods of Bible study, you also need to know the background and setting of a book of the Bible. Who wrote the book? Why was the book written? When was it written? What conditions surrounded the writing of the book? You can learn the history, geography, and culture that surrounded the writing of a book, and you can understand the political, economic, and social factors that influenced events in the Bible by consulting the writings of the experts and by making personal observations. This way to study the Bible is called background Bible study.

Topics for Background Bible Study

- History
- Geography
- Culture
- Sociology

Day 1
What to Look For

When you study **history**, you can learn either the background of an incident in a Bible book or the background from which a book of the Bible was written. If you study an event, you locate it in the life of a person or a nation. If you study a book of the Bible, you place it in a writer's life or in a nation's history.

You probably know that Paul wrote 1 Corinthians. But can you place Paul's contact with the Corinthians in the context of his life? What do you know about his experience at Corinth? A background study of Acts 18:1-17 will give you information to help place 1 Corinthians in the life of Paul.

Week 7

My brethren, count it all joy when ye fall into divers temptations; knowing this, that the trying of our faith worketh patience. But let patience have her perfect work, that ye may be perfect and entire, wanting nothing.

James 1:2-4, KJV

Week 4

Be careful for nothing; but in every thing by prayer and supplication with thanksgiving let your requests be made known unto God. And the peace of God, which passeth all understanding, shall keep your hearts and minds through Christ Jesus.

Philippians 4:6-7, KJV

Week 1

Be ye kind one to another, tenderhearted, forgiving one another, even as God for Christ's sake hath forgiven you.

Ephesians 4:32, KJV

Week 8

The very God of peace sanctify you wholly; and I pray God your whole spirit and soul and body be preserved blameless unto the coming of our Lord Jesus Christ.

1 Thessalonians 5:23, KJV

Week 5

Whosoever drinketh of the water that I shall give him shall never thirst; but the water that I shall give him shall be in him a well of water springing up into everlasting life.

John 4:14, KJV

Week 2

Casting all your care upon him; for he careth for you.

1 Peter 5:7, KJV

Week 9

Now we exhort you, brethren, warn them that are unruly, comfort the feebleminded, support the weak, be patient toward all men.

1 Thessalonians 5:14, KJV

Week 6

A new commandment I give unto you, that ye love one another; as I have loved you, that ye also love one another. By this shall all men know that ye are my disciples, if ye have love one to another.

John 13:34-35, KJV

Week 3

That I may know him, and the power of his resurrection, and the fellowship of his sufferings, being made conformable unto his death.

Philippians 3:10, KJV

Week 1

Ephesians 4:32, KJV

Week 4

Philippians 4:6-7, KJV

Week 7

James 1:2-4, KJV

Week 2

1 Peter 5:7, KJV

Week 5

John 4:14, KJV

Week 8

1 Thessalonians 5:23, KJV

Week 3

Philippians 3:10, KJV

Week 6

John 13:34-35, KJV

Week 9

1 Thessalonians 5:14, KJV

Week 7

Consider it all joy, my brethren, when you encounter various trials, knowing that the testing of your faith produces endurance. And let endurance have its perfect result, that you may be perfect and complete, lacking in nothing.

James 1:2-4, NASB

Week 4

Be anxious for nothing, but in everything by prayer and supplication with thanksgiving let your requests be made known to God. And the peace of God, which surpasses all comprehension, shall guard your hearts and your minds in Christ Jesus.

Philippians 4:6-7, NASB

Week 1

Be kind to one another, tender-hearted, forgiving each other, just as God in Christ also has forgiven you.

Ephesians 4:32, NASB

Week 8

May the God of peace Himself sanctify you entirely; and may your spirit and soul and body be preserved complete, without blame at the coming of our Lord Jesus Christ.

1 Thessalonians 5:23, NASB

Week 5

Whoever drinks of the water that I shall give him shall never thirst; but the water that I shall give him shall become in him a well of water springing up to eternal life.

John 4:14, NASB

Week 2

Casting all your anxiety upon Him, because He cares for you.

1 Peter 5:7, NASB

Week 9

We urge you, brethren, admonish the unruly, encourage the fainthearted, help the weak, be patient with all men.

1 Thessalonians 5:14, NASB

Week 6

A new commandment I give to you, that you love one another, even as I have loved you, that you also love one another. By this all men will know that you are My disciples, if you have love for one another.

John 13:34-35, NASB

Week 3

That I may know Him, and the power of His resurrection and the fellowship of His sufferings, being conformed to His death.

Philippians 3:10, NASB

Week 1

Ephesians 4:32, NASB

Week 4

Philippians 4:6-7, NASB

Week 7

James 1:2-4, NASB

Week 2

1 Peter 5:7, NASB

Week 5

John 4:14, NASB

Week 8

1 Thessalonians 5:23, NASB

Week 3

Philippians 3:10, NASB

Week 6

John 13:34-35, NASB

Week 9

1 Thessalonians 5:14, NASB

† Read Acts 18:1-17 to discover the answers to the following questions.

Who were Paul's friends? What were they like?

_____

_____

How did the Jews influence what Paul did in Corinth?

_____

_____

How did the Roman government influence what Paul did in Corinth?

_____

_____

How did God's leadership influence what Paul did in Corinth?

_____

_____

You have just done a background study that gives you information about Paul's contact with the Corinthians. In Corinth Paul stayed with his friends Aquila and Priscilla, who were believers and tent makers like Paul. Paul won many converts there. The Lord appeared to Paul and assured him of His presence, encouraging Paul to witness without fear. Paul continued to teach God's Word for 18 months, but the Jews united against Paul and brought him before the Roman proconsul Gallio. However, Gallio considered this a religious matter and refused to become involved. After a while Paul left Corinth and traveled to Syria.

Understanding Paul's experience in Corinth gives you important background information for interpreting 1 Corinthians.

Background Bible study also involves studying **geography** to visualize the physical backdrop for an event or a book in the Bible. You can learn the locations of cities and the significance of bodies of water such as rivers, lakes, and seas. You can discover the distances between important points, prominent features such as mountains, and the general influence of geography.

Let's look at how an understanding of geography sheds light on a Bible passage or prompts you to further study. John 4:3-4 records that Jesus "left Judea, and departed again into Galilee. And He had to pass through Samaria." The statement indicates that this is not the usual way Jews traveled between Galilee and Judea. Look at a map of Palestine in your Bible or in a Bible atlas or look at the following sketch.

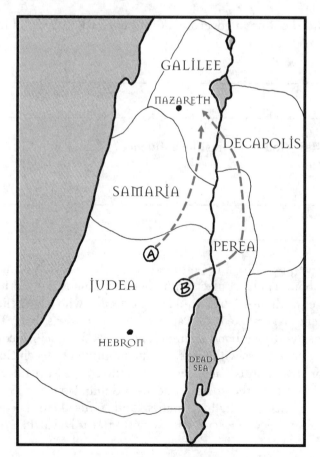

✝ What seems to be the logical, simplest, and most conven-
ient and direct way of traveling between Judea and Galilee?
❑ Route A   ❑ Route B

Are you surprised to know that although route A is more
direct, nearly all Jews used route B? In doing the unusual thing,
Jesus actually selected the most direct route. This means that all
those who used route B were enduring an unnecessary inconvenience. Why?

✝ Consult a commentary or another Bible-study aid to
learn why the Jews took the longer route. Briefly describe
what you found.

_____

_____

Do you see how an understanding of geography can prompt
you to do further study? The Jews selected the longer route to
avoid passing through the territory of the Samaritans, whom they
regarded with contempt. Your study of geography helps you
better understand Jesus' actions in John 4. Jesus traveled from
Judea to Galilee by passing through Samaria. This route took
Jesus into the territory where the multiracial Samaritans lived.
Jesus made contact with many Samaritans and led many to
believe in Him.

Learning about the **culture** of the people in the Bible is another
form of background Bible study that enriches interpretation.
Culture involves a study of the intellectual interests in a civiliza-
tion. It involves a knowledge of religion, science, music, art,
drama, literature, and philosophy.

A background study of the Bible also involves a study of
sociology. This is a study of group behavior and human relationships. This kind of study gives you information about families,
towns, cities, government, travel, business, and social classes.

As you perform background studies of the Bible, you use two
types of helps. First, you use the actual evidence from the Bible

itself, as you did earlier when you read Acts 18:1-17. Second, you use such tools as Bible dictionaries; encyclopedias; and various reference books on the Bible's history, geography, culture, and sociology. The need to do background Bible study is another reason it is important to build a library of Bible-study resources.

† Your Scripture-memory verse this week is John 4:14, which records good news Jesus delivered to the Samaritan woman. Begin memorizing this verse, using the Scripture-memory card at the center of your workbook.

Day 2
The Historical Background

An important part of background Bible study is exploring the historical context. The Bible writers wrote their messages in the middle of fast-breaking events in history. You can understand the books of the Bible more completely if you understand the history that lies behind them.

Many helpful tools present the historical background of a Bible book or an event. The books of the Bible contain information about the history of the times. Often an incident in the Book of Acts gives helpful insights about events in Paul's life and ministry. Many incidental comments in books of both Testaments provide a wealth of details about a book's historical background.

In addition to using the Bible itself, you will find that Bible dictionaries and encyclopedias give much assistance. Often these tools call attention to details in the Bible we might otherwise overlook. Both the Bible dictionary and the encyclopedia contain information about people, places, and events listed alphabetically.

Let's look at 1 Thessalonians to learn something about the historical background of that book. We first want to find out something about the city of Thessalonica. We also want to learn about the history of Paul's relationship with the city and the church. We are interested in obtaining information about the time in which Paul wrote the book.

✝ Use a Bible dictionary or encyclopedia to learn the following background information about Thessalonica.

Thessalonica was the capital of what Roman province?

_____

Why was Thessalonica an important city in its day?

_____

_____

I'm sure you had no trouble discovering that Thessalonica was the capital of the province of Macedonia. The city enjoyed great commercial success because of its strategic location at the junction of the land route from Italy to the East and the trade route from the Aegean to the Danube.

✝ Now study Acts 17:1-11 to discover information that will help you understand Paul's relationship with Thessalonica.

How did Paul begin his ministry there?

_____

_____

Who responded to Paul in Thessalonica?

_____

How did the Jews respond to Paul?

_____

_____

Your study should have revealed that Paul evangelized the city of Thessalonica against the opposition of the Jews and established a church there. Paul began his ministry by going to the synagogue and giving evidence that Jesus is the Christ. Many God-fearing Greeks and prominent women accepted Christ, but the Jews stirred up vehement opposition among the crowd and the city authorities.

Background study also teaches you when 1 Thessalonians was written.

✝ Read the parts of Acts immediately before and after Acts 17 that answer the following questions.

Where had Paul been before coming to Thessalonica?

_____

Where did he go after leaving Thessalonica?

_____

In Acts you learn that the events of chapter 17 took place during what we call Paul's second missionary journey. Paul had visited Philippi before coming to Thessalonica, and he went to Berea, Athens, and Corinth after leaving the city.

✝ Now consult in a Bible dictionary or encyclopedia the article "Thessalonians, First Epistle to." When does it date Paul's second missionary journey?

_____

How does the article date the writing of 1 Thessalonians?

_____

Most Bible dictionaries and encyclopedias indicate that Paul made his second missionary journey sometime between A.D. 50

and 53. They state that Paul probably wrote the letter of 1 Thessalonians after Timothy's return from Thessalonica to Corinth (see Acts 18:5; 1 Thessalonians 3:6). This is frequently dated around A.D. 51.

Here a combination of reading the Bible and using tools for Bible study provides additional insight into the historical background of 1 Thessalonians.

Day 3
The Geographical Background

This week you are studying background Bible study to gain more insight into the Bible's meaning. Yesterday you did a historical background study. Exploring the geographical background is another way to do background Bible study. Biblical geography involves studying the land in which the biblical events occurred. From a study of geography you can learn information about cities, lakes, seas, rivers, mountains, and the ways these geographical conditions affected people.

Generally, the Bible does not provide help for a person who needs to learn its geography. The writers of the Bible usually assumed that a reader understood the geographical features that were important in interpretation. Bible dictionaries and encyclopedias help by giving information on the geographical backgrounds of events recorded in the Bible. A city, a river, or a significant geographical feature mentioned by name in the Bible appears under that name in these study tools.

A Bible atlas provides much help in Bible study. Its maps assist in the location of unfamiliar cities. It also gives information about the distances between biblical locations.

The rapidly developing science of biblical archaeology provides assistance in describing life in Bible times. Archaeologists have excavated entire biblical cities such as Corinth. Thus, much information about life during Bible times has become available. This archaeological information frequently appears in Bible dictionaries and encyclopedias. It may also appear in Bible commentaries.

Whenever events in a biblical situation involve movement from one place to another, it is helpful to discover information about the places and areas involved. This type of study leads to a better understanding of a Scripture passage. After you have used study helps to obtain the geographical information, it is useful to summarize the effect the information has on the passage you are studying.

✝ Read Acts 13:13. Mark the following statement T for true or F for false.
___ The Bible clearly states the reason John Mark returned to Jerusalem.

In Acts 13:13 John Mark left Paul and Barnabas on the first missionary journey in Perga of Pamphylia. The Bible does not mention anything unusual about the geographical terrain around Perga. However, an article dealing with Perga in Bible dictionaries or encyclopedias indicates that Perga was a reasonably flat seaport where the disease of malaria was common. To stay in Perga could lead to illness. Inland from Perga the Taurus Mountains quickly rose to about 3,600 feet at some points. This was a bandit-infested region and was dangerous and difficult for travelers.

Why did John Mark leave Paul and Barnabas? The Bible does not clearly state the reason, but the area's unpleasant geographical features may have played a part in his decision.

In Genesis 11:31 Abraham moved with his father, Terah, from Ur of the Chaldeans to the city of Haran. Abraham was living in Haran when he received God's call to leave for the Promised Land. Information about the city of Haran suggests that it was located on a prominent trade route between Babylonia and the Mediterranean Sea. In ancient times it was a center of idolatrous and pagan worship.

✝ Study a map in your Bible or in a Bible atlas or the sketch on page 105. What does a knowledge of geography and of the customs of the time tell you about Abraham's journey from Haran to the Promised Land?

_____

_____

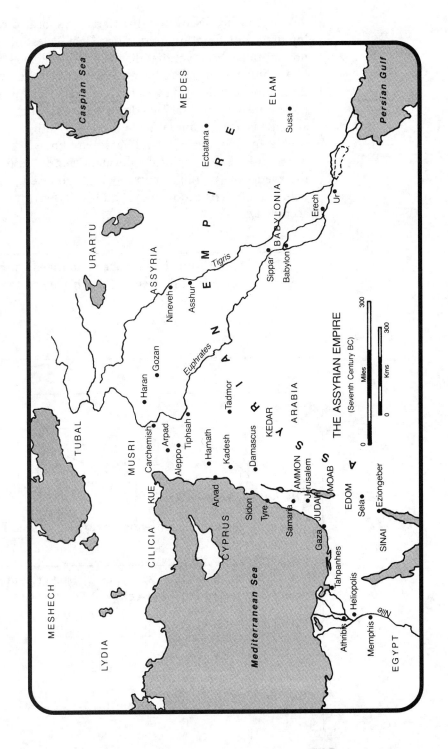

THE ASSYRIAN EMPIRE
(Seventh Century BC)

You probably discovered that Haran was located between three hundred and four hundred miles from Palestine. It would be normal today to travel that distance. In Abraham's day, however, it was highly unusual and would be equivalent to traveling many thousands of miles today. To have relocated that distance is even more unusual. In Abraham's day a man most often lived and died among his own people. What a display of faith it was to leave his people and to move to a land he did not know!

The use of geographical information in biblical study makes the events of the Bible more vivid. A knowledge of geography helps a student understand and interpret the Bible more accurately.

✝ **By this point you should have memorized your Scripture-memory verse for this week. Write it here from memory.**

_____

_____

_____

_____

Day 4
The Cultural Background

This week you are learning how to do background Bible study.

✝ **Can you name the two types of background study you have learned so far this week?**

1. _____

2. _____

You have already learned to do historical and geographical background studies. Today you will learn how to explore the cultural background of the Bible.

Biblical culture involves a study of the cultural environment in which the biblical writers lived. This area is broad, including religion, science, literature, music, and many other areas of knowledge and art. A knowledge of biblical culture adds life and interest to your understanding of the Bible. It also assists you in making your interpretation of the Bible accurate and clear.

The sources of help for the study of Bible culture include Bible commentaries, which provide specific cultural information on passages of Scripture. The previously mentioned Bible dictionaries and encyclopedias are other tools for discovering cultural information.

A knowledge of Bible culture makes your Bible study more vivid and accurate. For example, learning information about the Sadducees and the Pharisees makes many of Jesus' words about them clearer. What did they teach and believe? Why did Jesus denounce their hypocrisy so strongly? You can find information about these groups by looking under the proper article in a Bible dictionary or encyclopedia. After you have found the information, you will want to summarize how the information will aid in your interpretation of the Bible.

Let's look at two examples of the way a knowledge of culture can enhance your understanding of the Bible. In John 2:18 the Jews challenged Jesus to produce evidence of His authority to drive the money changers from the temple. His response to them was " 'Destroy this temple, and in three days I will raise it up.' " Jesus referred to His body as the temple. His hearers thought He was referring to their beautiful temple. The Jews' response to Jesus' words in verse 20 was, " 'It took forty-six years to build this temple, and will You raise it up in three days?' " What was this temple they described?

✝ Study John 2:13-22 in a commentary or look up "Temple of Herod" or "Herod's temple" in a Bible dictionary or a Bible encyclopedia. See what you can discover about the temple the people thought Jesus was talking about. Write at the top of page 108 what you learn.

_____

_____

_____

_____

For centuries the Jews had a small, fortress-like temple for their use in worship. It was started under the Old Testament leader Zerubbabel (see Ezra 3:8), but it was not as beautiful as Solomon's temple. Herod the Great, who had reigned over Palestine from 37 to 4 B.C., wanted to expand this temple into a magnificent temple by which the Jews would remember him. He started his project around 20 B.C., and the completion of the task required many years. The actual work had lasted for 46 years at the time of the conversation between Jesus and the Jews.

The Jews were so devoted to this temple that a threat against it seemed blasphemous to them. When the Jews felt that Jesus was threatening their temple, they used it as a reason for encouraging His death (see Matthew 27:40).

Acts 17:18 also illustrates the way understanding the culture can clarify a Bible passage. This verse records that Paul preached the resurrection to some Epicurean and Stoic philosophers in Athens. What these groups believed had a definite influence on the way they heard what Paul was saying. However, the Bible gives no indication of what those groups believed.

✝ Use a Bible dictionary or encyclopedia to discover what Stoics and Epicureans believed. Summarize what you learn.

What Stoics believed: _____

_____

_____

_____

What Epicureans believed: _____

_____

_____

_____

_____

Epicureans felt that a person ought to be satisfied with the simple pleasures of life. These simple pleasures ought to bring happiness and peace. Stoics felt that a person ought to show courage and bravery in accepting the events of life. When Paul made his appeal to his audience in Acts 17:28, he used language the Stoics could understand. The Stoics were more prepared to accept the existence of a loving God who would meet their needs. The Epicureans felt that a person's future was limited to earth and depended on himself. Paul was trying to reach the Stoics who would listen.

Do you see how a knowledge of the cultural background enhances your understanding of the Bible? Background Bible study brings to life concepts and topics that would otherwise seem obscure or confusing to modern readers. Tomorrow you will learn another valuable way to study the background of the Bible.

Day 5
The Sociological Background

This week you have learned how background Bible study can illuminate the historical, geographical, and cultural surroundings in which the Bible was written. Today you will learn the final area in which background Bible study can increase your understanding of the Bible. That area is the sociological background. Sociology is the study of all types of human relationships. It includes the study of relationships in families, communities, governments, business, races, and religions. Such tools as a Bible dictionary and a Bible encyclopedia provide sociological information about the Bible.

To discover the sociological background of the Bible, you must find information on the particular institution or practice the Bible is describing. After you have collected the information, you can summarize its effect on and meaning for the passage.

A study of the Book of Philemon reveals information about the practice of slavery in the first century and the church's attitude toward it. Information about these practices appears in Bible dictionaries or encyclopedias.

> ✝ Read the article "Philemon, Epistle to" in a Bible diction-ary, encyclopedia, or commentary. Write what you learn about the sociological background that enhances your understanding of the Book of Philemon.

_____

_____

_____

_____

_____

_____

_____

The Book of Philemon deals with the runaway slave Onesimus, who was owned by Philemon. Legally, an owner could brutally punish a runaway.

Roman law suggested that whoever hosted a runaway was liable to pay the owner for each day of lost work time. When Paul told Philemon to charge to him anything Onesimus owed, he may have been promising that he would repay Philemon for the time when Onesimus was a runaway (see Philemon 18).

Slaves generally had no rights of their own. They were treated as property. Yet Paul asked for humane treatment for Onesimus and even dropped a hint that Philemon might free him (see Philemon 21). Paul did not denounce slavery, but he established an attitude in the church in which slavery would slowly die out.

Matthew 1:18-25 is another passage that can best be understood by considering the sociological background.

✝ Read about the marriage practices in Mary and Joseph's time by looking in a Bible dictionary and encyclopedia under articles such as "Marriage," "Mary," or "Joseph," or in a commentary. Describe Joseph's options when he was faced with Mary's pregnancy.

_____

_____

_____

During the engagement Joseph would have worked to accumulate a dowry to give to the father-in-law. This normally required about a year, depending on the wealth and income of the prospective groom. During this period Joseph learned about Mary's pregnancy. The passage states that Joseph considered breaking his engagement to Mary when he learned that she was pregnant.

In Jewish culture the breakup of an engaged couple was similar to divorce in our society. Joseph could have settled the divorce publicly with disgrace and potential punishment for Mary. Joseph's kind, merciful spirit led him to reject a public procedure that could humiliate Mary. He also had the option of privately delivering to Mary a statement that he planned to divorce her. Joseph decided that he wanted to handle the divorce privately. While Joseph was considering this, an angel from God led him to consider completing the marriage. That was the course he followed. A sociological study gives you background knowledge that helps you understand this Bible passage more fully.

Congratulations. You have completed this week's examination of background Bible study.

† See if you can name the four areas of background study you have practiced this week.

1. _____

2. _____

3. _____

4. _____

We hope your mastery of background Bible study has made you aware that the Bible is grounded in reality. It reflects actual historical events, geographical locations, cultures, and sociological relationships. Exploring the background of Bible passages brings rich new dimensions to your understanding of the Bible's meaning and message.

† Review your Scripture-memory assignment for this week by writing it here.

_____

_____

Briefly describe what this verse means to you after reciting and meditating on it this week.

_____

_____

Review the previous weeks' Scripture-memory verses.

† Close this week's study in prayer. Thank God for revealing Himself through the reality of His creation.

Week 6

How to Apply Bible Study: Biographical Bible Study

Day 1
Areas to Apply the Bible

Day 2
Purposes and Principles of Biographical Bible Study

Day 3
Doing a Biographical Bible Study

Day 4
Applying a Biographical Bible Study

Day 5
Purposes and Principles of Character-Trait Bible Study

Over the past three weeks you studied and practiced synthetic Bible study, analytical Bible study, and background Bible study. Now you begin a two-week study of how to apply the Bible. These will be important studies for your Christian walk, because the purpose of all Scripture study is to lead you to apply it to your life.

Recall the five principles for applying the Bible that you studied in week 2.

Principles for Applying the Bible

1. Apply the Bible according to its real meaning.
2. Use the Bible as a Book of principles.
3. Use the promises properly.
4. Use a cross-cultural understanding.
5. Use the Bible wisely.

These principles will guide you to interpret God's Word correctly as you seek ways to apply it to your life.

For example, John mentioned that Jesus "had to pass through Samaria" (John 4:4). John was not saying that God forced Jesus to go through Samaria. He meant that Jesus chose to ignore the Jews' prejudice toward the Samaritans and to take the most direct route from Judea to Galilee. The application to us is to conduct our lives with an openness to opportunities to serve God. As Jesus passed through Samaria, He found such an opportunity with the woman at the well.

You may apply the Bible to many different situations of life. You must be certain, however, to base your application on a right interpretation of God's message.

Day 1
Areas to Apply the Bible

Today you will learn how to apply the Bible to four areas.
1. To your relationship with God
2. To your own life

SCRIPTURE-MEMORY VERSE
A new commandment I give to you, that you love one another, even as I have loved you, that you also love one another. By this all men will know that you are My disciples, if you have love for one another.
John 13:34-35

3. To your relationships with others
4. To the church

First, apply the Bible to your relationship with God. This relationship is vertical because you relate upward to God in obedience to Him. The Bible may tell you something to believe about God, Jesus Christ, the Holy Spirit, sin, forgiveness, or eternal life. It may describe something you are to do for God, such as choosing a vocation or making a special use of time.

Areas to Apply the Bible

1. Your relationship with God
2. Your own life
3. Your relationships with others
4. The church

✝ Read Colossians 3:17. Check the statement that most closely states the meaning of this verse.
❑ Your words are not important as long as you do good deeds in Jesus' name.
❑ Practice all of your beliefs and actions with a desire to glorify God.

This verse tells you to practice all of your beliefs and actions with a desire to glorify God.

Second, you may apply the Bible to yourself personally. The Bible shows you personal sins you must confess to God. It describes attitudes you must forsake. It challenges you to experience contentment, joy, obedience, and love as you live for God.

✝ Read 1 John 1:7-9. Why is confessing your sins necessary for walking in the light?

_____

_____

As you confess your sins to God, you are able to live in a relationship of peace and harmony with Him and with others.

Third, you may apply the Bible to your relationships with others. These relationships are horizontal because you relate across personal boundaries, from one person to another. The Bible may call you to show forgiveness to members of your family, to your fellow workers, to your fellow students, or to your neighbors. The Bible can call you to express Christ's love to your enemies, your closest friends, and your casual contacts.

✝ **Read today's Scripture-memory verse, John 13:34-35. How do we show others that we are Christ's servants?**

_____

_____

Our love for one another demonstrates to others that we belong to Christ.

Finally, apply the Bible to the church, God's people on earth. The church must demonstrate God's love, grace, and compassion for those who need to know Christ.

✝ **Read Ephesians 4:11-16 and fill in the following blanks. The church is a place where believers—**
- are equipped for the work of _____;
- build up the _____ of Christ;
- attain to the _____ of the faith and of the knowledge of the _____ of God;
- grow to the measure of the stature of the fullness of _____;
- speak the truth in _____;
- grow up in all aspects into the head, who is _____.

Ephesians 4:11-16 describes the church as a fellowship where God's people are equipped for spiritual service. God wants the church to reflect His purity and holiness to others. As you read the Scriptures, you can apply its message to bring the church into this image and purpose.

As you read the Scriptures, try to apply its message to these four areas. The areas overlap, for when you learn something about God you often learn something about yourself, your relationships with others, and the church. Being alert to these four areas helps you be specific as you apply the Bible.

✝ Reread John 13:34-35, which you read earlier today. Pray about and meditate on these verses. Then write ways to apply this passage to the four areas on the chart "How I Can Apply John 13:34-35."

How I Can Apply John 13:34-35	
To My Relationship with God	**To My Life**
To My Relationships with Others	**To the Church**

John 13:34-35 is also your Scripture-memory passage for this week. Start memorizing these verses, using the Scripture-memory card at the center of your workbook.

Day 2
Purposes and Principles of Biographical Bible Study

Yesterday you considered four areas of life in which you can apply the Bible.

✝ **Can you recall the four areas of application you studied yesterday?**

1. _____

2. _____

3. _____

4. _____

You learned that you can apply the Bible to your relationship with God, to your own life, to your relationships with others, and to the church. During the next two weeks you will learn methods of Bible study that will help you apply the Bible to all four areas. These methods are biographical Bible study, character-trait Bible study, and devotional Bible study.

Biographical study is a method that examines the lives of the people in the Bible. Biographical study of the Bible has much appeal because people are interested in others' experiences. The people of the Bible demonstrate actions we can imitate and faults we must avoid. We can look at one incident in the life of a Bible character, or we can survey the entire life.

✝ **Read the following Scriptures and summarize the reasons God gave us the Old Testament accounts.**

1 Corinthians 10:1-13: _____

_____

117

Romans 15:4: _____

_____

The verses from 1 Corinthians indicate that God gave the Old Testament accounts to serve as examples for us. Paul reminds us in Romans 15:4 that "whatever was written in earlier times was written for our instruction." The purpose of biographical study of the Bible is to learn the lessons God has shown through His people in the past. In the Bible we find numerous people—men and women, good and bad—whose lives we can examine in detail.

The tools you need for biographical study are a Bible, a concordance, and a Bible dictionary or encyclopedia. Here is the general process you will follow.

1. Read relevant passages about the person in the Scriptures.
2. Read in a Bible dictionary or encyclopedia an article about the character you are studying.
3. Interpret the information you have collected and apply it to the four areas of application you have studied: your relationship with God, your own life, your relationships with others, and the church.

You will have opportunities to practice this method later in the week, but today we want to introduce you to four foundational principles for doing biographical Bible study.

1. _Begin with a simple character._ Some people of the Bible, such as Barnabas, Priscilla, and Aquila, appear only a few times. Other characters, such as Moses, David, and Paul, are so important that you will not be able to study their lives quickly. Begin with a simple character and work up to a more complex character.
2. _Watch for name changes and confusion of identity._ The Bible contains the stories of several people with the names of Mary, James, and John. As you study these people, be sure that you are studying the right character. Some people of the Bible are known by more than one name. Mark, the author of the second Gospel, is known as John, Mark, or Marcus, and many books speak of him as John Mark. To gather all of the facts about people mentioned with more than one name, learn the names the Bible writers use for them. Usually a

glance at a Bible dictionary, encyclopedia, or concordance can give you this information.

✝ Discover the number of times each of the following names appears in the Bible.

Mark: _____   James: _____
John: _____   Zechariah: _____

Discover by what other names the following persons were known.

Silas: _____

Peter: _____

Paul: _____

Jacob: _____

Principles for Biographical Bible Study

1. Begin with a simple character.
2. Watch for name changes and confusion of identity.
3. Extend your exploration beyond a name search in a concordance.
4. Use your imagination vividly.

---

3. *Extend your exploration beyond a name search in a concordance.* In the Books of 1 and 2 Timothy we can learn a lot about Timothy even in sections where his name is not mentioned. Paul wrote both books to him. Information about Joshua appears throughout the entire Book of Joshua, even in those paragraphs in which Joshua's name may be absent.

4. *Use your imagination vividly.* Learn about the customs and culture in which the persons lived. Try to imagine how they felt and thought. Observe how they responded to

circumstances. This will demand that you repeatedly read the Scriptures about the characters and think about them. As you study the characters, do not look for outside help in understanding their lives until you have thought about them. Using a Bible dictionary or encyclopedia too early will rob you of the freshness and the joy of discovering what God wants to show you through your personal experience with His Word.

✝ Review the principles of biographical study that you studied today. Then try to summarize the principles by filling in the blanks.
1. Begin with a _____ character.
2. Watch for _____ changes and confusion of _____.
3. Extend your exploration beyond a _____ _____ in a concordance.
4. Use your _____ vividly.

Tomorrow you will practice these principles by completing a biographical Bible study.

Day 3
Doing a Biographical Bible Study

You are ready to learn how to complete a biographical study of a Bible character. As you read the following steps, refer to the chart "Biographical Bible Study" on page 122. Later you will fill in the chart when it is time to practice.
1. *Select a character for study.* You will want to choose someone whose strengths you admire and whose failures you want to avoid. Begin with a character whose life is simple enough to analyze easily. You will write the character's name at the top of the chart.
2. *List Scripture references.* Use a concordance to find all of the references about that person. If possible, list every verse in which the name of the person appears.

3. *Use the Bible to learn all you can about the person.* You may find information about that person's birth, life, and death. Record the person's history and life setting. For example, if you study Barnabas, you may want to find out something about the missionary journey he made with Paul (see Acts 13—14). Later you may want to read articles in a Bible dictionary or encyclopedia about the events during your subject's lifetime, but start with the Scripture references you have listed to find information about the person. You will record your information adjacent to the applicable Scripture references you have listed on the chart.

4. *List observations about the person.* Your observations may include questions or problems for which you want answers. Some of your questions may lead you to do more research later, but for now, record only the observations that arise from the Scripture references you have listed. You will write them adjacent to the related references on the chart.

✝ **Stop and practice. Make a copy of the chart "Biographical Bible Study" on page 122 to use in a biographical study of John Mark by following the steps outlined so far.**

Are you satisfied that you have completed that much of your assignment as well as possible? Good! Work on your own today. Tomorrow we will give you a chance to compare your work with some of the possibilities we see.

5. *Write an outline of the person's life.* Include as much about the person's life as you have been able to discover. Sometimes you can formulate a chronological outline of the person's life. Sometimes your outline consists of the places in which he lived—a geographical outline. You may not have enough information to make a clear outline, but an effort to use what you have will be helpful. Studying Paul's life, for example, becomes more meaningful when you divide his life into his three missionary journeys and his imprisonment. That way you can observe the changes and developments in each section of his life.

Biographical Bible Study

Bible Character _____

Scripture References	Biographical Information	Observations	Life Outline	Character Traits	Summary

✝ Outline as much as you can of John Mark's life. Write your outline in the appropriate column on the chart "Biographical Bible Study."

6. *Identify positive character traits or failures to avoid.* Among the items you may want to observe are general reputation, aims and motives, family and national background, relationships and actions with other people, and general personality and spiritual life. List these traits in the appropriate column on the chart.

✝ Stop and list John Mark's character traits in the appropriate column of the chart "Biographical Bible Study."

7. *Briefly summarize what you have learned from the person's life.*

✝ In the last column on the chart "Biographical Bible Study," write a brief summary of what you have learned from your study of John Mark's life.

8. *Apply the lesson you have learned.* You will not practice this step today, but tomorrow you will learn how to apply this lesson to your relationship with God, to your own life, to your relationships with others, and to the church.

Doing a Biographical Bible Study

1. Select a character for study.
2. List Scripture references.
3. Use the Bible to learn all you can about the person.
4. List observations about the person.
5. Write an outline of the person's life.
6. Identify positive character traits or failures to avoid.
7. Briefly summarize what you have learned from the person's life.
8. Apply the lesson you have learned.

✝ By now you should have memorized your Scripture-memory verses for this week. Write them here from memory.

_____

_____

_____

_____

Day 4
Applying a Biographical Bible Study

You are in the process of learning how to do biographical Bible study as a way of applying the Bible. Yesterday you found all of the references to the life of John Mark that appear in the New Testament. You recorded information, made preliminary observations about him, outlined as much of his life as possible, listed character traits, and summarized lessons to be learned from his life. We want to provide some information about John Mark so that you can check and possibly improve your work. See if the work you did yesterday on the chart "Biographical Bible Study" (p. 122) includes the information and answers the questions that follow.

John Mark is mentioned as Mark in Acts 12:12,25; 15:37,39; Colossians 4:10; 2 Timothy 4:11; Philemon 24; and 1 Peter 5:13. He is mentioned as John in Acts 13:5,13, and the name John also appears in the previously mentioned Scriptures of Acts 12:12,25 and 15:37.

As you reflected on these verses, did you observe that in Acts 12:12 Mark's family home was used in a prayer meeting for Peter's release from jail? Is Mark's father mentioned? What does this indicate about the influence of Mark's father on the son? What size home was probably needed to host the praying Christians? What does this show about the wealth of Mark's family?

In Acts 13:5 Mark left on Paul's first missionary journey. Mark is described as a helper. What does this indicate about the kind of role Mark had?

In Acts 13:13 Mark left Paul and Barnabas for unexplained reasons. What does the terrain around the town of Perga suggest as possible reasons for leaving Paul and Barnabas? See yesterday's study for answers to these questions.

In Acts 15:37-41 Paul and Barnabas disagreed over the question of taking Mark on the second missionary journey. What does the description of this discussion suggest about the intensity of their feelings? What happened to Paul and Silas after they began the second missionary journey?

Notice the gracious descriptions of Mark given by Paul in Philemon 24; Colossians 4:10; and 2 Timothy 4:11. In what area of ministry does Mark's most significant ability seem to lie? What do these verses indicate about Paul's willingness to admit that he had made a mistake?

Notice the reference to the relationship between Barnabas and Mark in Colossians 4:10. What attitude does Barnabas show in his defense of and work with Mark?

Can you assign possible dates in Paul's ministry to the passages in Philemon 24; Colossians 4:10; and 2 Timothy 4:11? Are they Paul's earliest or latest opinions of Mark? What insight into the potential usefulness of Mark does the reference in 1 Peter 5:13 show?

Was it difficult or easy to develop an outline of Mark's life? No particular outline is correct to the exclusion of all others. Compare your outline to the following one.

1. Mark's home background and early life—Acts 12:12
2. Mark's opportunity for service—Acts 12:25; 13:5
3. Mark's failure—Acts 13:13; 15:37-39
4. Mark's comeback—Colossians 4:10; Philemon 24;
    2 Timothy 4:11; 1 Peter 5:13

What general traits of character did you observe in the life of John Mark? How did his early life affect him? What attitudes are reflected in Acts 13:13? What character traits appear in the later references to him in Colossians 4:10; Philemon 24; 2 Timothy 4:11; and 1 Peter 5:13?

✝ Check your evaluation of John Mark's character by briefly surveying an article about him in a Bible dictionary or encyclopedia.

One fact that may come to your attention is that church tradition says that John Mark was stump-fingered. This may mean that he lost a finger in an accident or was born without one.

How did you do? Don't be disappointed or frustrated. If you had done a perfect job, you would have no reason to study these sessions on biographical study, would you?

✝ Take time to change or add to the information on the chart you completed yesterday.

Now that you have studied the life of John Mark, it is time for you to determine what application you can make. Remember, Bible study is always to be applied to life. God's Word comes alive when you let it speak in your daily walk with God and in your relationships. Be sure that your application is specific and feasible. Make it something you can do.

✝ Using a copy of the chart "How I Can Apply a Biographical Study" on page 127, write applications from the life of John Mark that you will try to make to your relationship with God, to your own life, to your relationships with others, and to the church. Your statements should be clear, feasible, and specific.

When you have completed the various applications from the life of the person you study, you may want to check your study by comparing it with other helps. For example, if you study the life of Caleb in the Old Testament, check a Bible dictionary or encyclopedia for a good summary of his life. If your sources strongly suggest a trait you have overlooked or question a trait you have found, review your own interpretation.

How I Can Apply a Biographical Study

**To My Relationship
with God**

To My Life

**To My Relationships
with Others**

To the Church

How do you feel about biographical Bible study now that you have practiced it? It can be a time-consuming but very rewarding way to learn and apply lessons from God's Word. Tomorrow you will begin learning another method you can use to apply the Bible to your life.

Day 5
Purposes and Principles of Character-Trait Bible Study

Yesterday you completed your study of biographical Bible study. Today you will begin learning how to apply another kind of Bible study to your relationship with God, to your own life, to your relationships with others, and to the church. That method is character-trait Bible study.

One aim in Christian living is to produce godly character traits in your life. Character-trait Bible study attempts to identify the specific traits the Bible commends and denounces. Then you can apply God's power to produce the positive traits and avoid the negative traits. Your ultimate goal in this type of Bible study is to become more and more like the Lord Jesus.

Character-trait Bible study involves discovering what the Bible teaches about a particular trait. It has much in common with other types of Bible study such as biographical study and word study. It differs from biographical study in that you study traits or qualities rather than a person's entire life.

The tools you will need to carry out character-trait Bible study include a Bible, a concordance, and a Bible dictionary or a word-study book such as A. T. Robertson and James Swanson's *Word Pictures in the New Testament*. In addition, a topical Bible such as John Perry's *So That's in the Bible* may prove helpful. An English dictionary will be valuable. Also, you will need to understand the meanings of the following words.

✝ **Write the definition of each word.**

A synonym is _____

_____

An antonym is _____

_____

If you are not sure about your definitions, check them in a dictionary.

As you carry out character-trait Bible study, remember these guidelines.

1. *Select a character trait in which you have a vital interest.* The trait may be one you already have but need to develop more fully. Don't focus on the trait because you are merely curious. Study a specific trait you genuinely want to improve.

† **What are two character traits you would like to develop in your life?**

1. _____

2. _____

Name one negative character trait in your life you would like to learn about so that you can deal with it more effectively.

_____

2. *Concentrate on one quality at a time.* Concentrating on one quality is like hunting with a powerful rifle. With that rifle you can drill one shot into your prey in order to down it. Concentrating on many traits is like hunting with a shotgun. You may spray the entire forest with buckshot, but you may not bag a single animal. When you focus on a single trait, you can take the time to make certain that you are solidly building this trait into your life.

† **Which character trait would you study first?**

_____

3. *Study with the prayerful anticipation that God will produce the trait's good features in you.* Don't be disappointed if the trait is difficult to master. Fiery tempers and loose tongues do not develop overnight. Neither will a solution to these character deficiencies appear quickly. Focus on the specific trait you need and continue with a prayer for and study of the trait until it is a part of your life.

✝ When you study the trait you selected as your first choice, what results do you expect that study to produce?

_____

_____

4. *Realize that some of your negative qualities may be positive traits that are misused.* An undisciplined waste of time may actually reflect a disposition to show such compassion to others that you forget about the clock.

✝ Is it possible that your negative trait you identified earlier is a positive trait misused? ❑ Yes ❑ No If so, how can you correct the misuse?

_____

_____

5. *Recognize that some of the positive qualities in your life may reflect a natural personality rather than a deep spiritual conviction.* A gentleness of outlook and disposition may come from a casual, lazy attitude that lacks initiative. The gentle spirit is good, but it needs to be based more specifically on a positive response to God's character.

Do not view character-trait Bible study as merely an effort to master facts in the Bible. View it as a means God can use to produce traits in your life that are pleasing to Him. You will learn more about how to use this valuable method of study next week.

Guidelines for Character-Trait Bible Study

1. Select a character trait in which you have a vital interest.
2. Concentrate on one quality at a time.
3. Study with the prayerful anticipation that God will produce the trait's good features in you.
4. Realize that some of your negative qualities may be positive traits that are misused.
5. Recognize that some of the positive qualities in your life may reflect a natural personality rather than a deep spiritual conviction.

✝ Find someone who will listen to you quote this week's Scripture-memory passage and will check your recall against the verses in the Bible or on your Scripture-memory card.

Review the ways you applied these verses on paper at the end of day 1, page 116. Write one way you have already applied them to your life this week.

_____

_____

Review the previous weeks' Scripture-memory verses.

✝ Close this week's study in prayer. Thank God for His transforming Word and commit to Him to spend more time reading and meditating on His Word.

Week 7

How to Apply Bible Study: Character-Trait and Devotional Bible Study

Day 1
Using Bible References to Study Character Traits

Day 2
Using Bible Personalities to Study Character Traits

Day 3
Purposes and Principles of Devotional Bible Study

Day 4
Applying a Devotional Bible Study

Day 5
Practicing a Devotional Bible Study

SCRIPTURE-MEMORY VERSE
Consider it all joy, my brethren, when you encounter various trials, knowing that the testing of your faith produces endurance. And let endurance have its perfect result, that you may be perfect and complete, lacking in nothing.
James 1:2-4

Today you will begin your second week of examining methods for applying Bible study. Last week you completed biographical Bible study and were introduced to the major principles involved in character-trait Bible study.

This week you will do a character-trait Bible study, applying it to your relationship with God, your own life, your relationships with others, and the church. Beginning with day 3 you will learn and practice devotional Bible study. This method encourages you to make meaningful application of the Bible to your life and will transform your life.

Day 1
Using Bible References to Study Character Traits

Today you will practice doing a character-trait Bible study. You will also practice applying it to the four areas you studied last week: your relationship with God, your own life, your relationships with others, and the church.

As you read the following steps, refer to the worksheet "Character-Trait Bible Study" on pages 134-135. Do not complete the worksheet yet. You will use it today to practice character-trait Bible study.

1. *Select a trait.* Identify the trait you want to study.
2. *Record the dictionary meaning.* Find and write the meaning of the word using a dictionary.
3. *List synonyms.* Examining synonyms can help you understand the quality.
4. *List antonyms.* If you have a dictionary that gives antonyms, it can be very helpful. Some traits may have two or more opposites. For example, the opposite of joy could be sorrow, worry, self-pity, or even resentment.
5. *Discover the Bible definition of and teachings about the trait.* Use a concordance or a topical Bible to list references of Scripture passages in which the word appears. Study each passage and write a brief statement of what that passage says about the trait.
6. *Summarize the Bible teachings.* Write a brief summary of the Bible teachings you discovered about this trait. Your

summary may include information on how to produce or avoid this trait, as well as a statement from Scripture commenting on this trait.

7. *Reflect on your study.* Use the following questions to guide your thinking.
   - What are some benefits of this trait in my life and in the lives of others?
   - What are some problems this trait could produce in my life or in the lives of others?
   - Is there a promise or warning from God about this trait? If so, what is it?
   - What factors produce this trait?
   - What effect does this trait produce in the life of the church?
   - Is this trait a part of God's character?

8. *Write applications.* Identify ways you can apply your study of this trait to your relationship with God, to your own life, to your relationships with others, and to the church.

Doing a Character-Trait Bible Study

1. Select a trait.
2. Record the dictionary meaning.
3. List synonyms.
4. List antonyms.
5. Discover the Bible definition of and teachings about the trait.
6. Summarize the Bible teachings.
7. Reflect on your study.
8. Write applications.

✝ Use the process you just examined to do a study of patience or endurance. Complete the worksheet "Character-Trait Bible Study" on pages 134-135. (A master copy of this worksheet can be found on pages 219-220.)

Character-Trait Bible Study

Trait: _____

Dictionary definition: _____

_____

Synonyms: _____

Antonyms: _____

Bible definition and teachings: _____

_____

Summary of Bible teachings: _____

_____

Reflections:

• What are some benefits of this trait in my life and in the lives of others?

_____

_____

• What are some problems this trait could produce in my life or in the lives of others?

_____

_____

• Is there a promise or warning from God about this trait? If so, what is it?

_____

• What factors produce this trait? _____

_____

• What effect does this trait produce in the life of the church?

_____

_____

• Is this trait a part of God's character? ❏ Yes ❏ No

Ways to apply the study—

• to my relationship with God: _____

_____

• to my own life: _____

_____

• to my relationships with others: _____

_____

• to the church: _____

_____

A dictionary defines *patience* as *the state of bearing pain or trials without complaint.* Other synonyms for the words are *steadfastness, perseverance,* and *stamina.* The opposite qualities include *impatience, instability*, and *wavering.*

The synonyms for *patience, perseverance,* and *endurance* are used several times in the New Testament. For example, in Luke 8:15 *perseverance* is used to describe those who hear the Word and bear fruit. In Romans 5:3 Paul writes that tribulation brings about perseverance. James 1:3 teaches "that the testing of your faith produces endurance." Finally, Romans 15:4 teaches that perseverance and the encouragement of the Scriptures bring hope to a believer's life.

In applying the scriptural teachings you discovered, you may have asked questions like these: What spiritual benefit does patience produce? How does this affect my attitude toward trials in life? What can happen in the life of a Christian who does not have patience? What are the means of producing patience in my life? Can I ever have too much of this trait? How does God show this trait? What will this trait cause in my relationship to myself? To others?

Accompany each step in your study of patience or endurance with a prayer that God will develop the trait in you. As you study the trait, God can make its experience a reality in your relationships with Him, with yourself, with others, and with the church.

✝ You may have read James 1:2-4 today as part of your character-trait study of patience. Those verses are your Scripture-memory passage for this week. Use the Scripture-memory card at the center of your workbook to begin learning these verses.

Day 2
Using Bible Personalities to Study Character Traits

Yesterday you learned to use Bible references to study traits of character. In addition to using specific Bible references, you can examine the lives of Bible characters to study traits. This method of study is similar to biographical study, but it differs in that you primarily study a single trait or characteristic.

The method for using a Bible character to study a trait is identical to the method for using Bible references. First you select the quality you want to study and find its definition in a dictionary. After you have listed a definition of the word, you also list synonyms and antonyms. Then you are ready to look for characters in the Bible who illustrate the trait you are studying.

How can you find the names of Bible characters who show the trait you are studying? Sometimes you can draw from your general knowledge of the Bible. You may be surprised at the ease with which you can associate different Bible characters with specific character traits.

✝ Match the traits on the right with the Bible characters on the left by placing the appropriate letter beside each name.

___	1. Job	a. love
___	2. Achan	b. deceit
___	3. Sapphira	c. encouragement
___	4. Saul	d. devotion
___	5. John	e. greed
___	6. Ruth	f. wisdom
___	7. Peter	g. patience
___	8. Barnabas	h. benevolence
___	9. Elijah	i. instability
___	10. Solomon	j. forgiveness
___	11. Hosea	k. courage
___	12. Dorcas	l. jealousy

How did you do? Answers are at the end of today's lesson.

Sometimes you can use a concordance to find specific passages that discuss the trait you are studying. Often these passages contain the name of a person who demonstrates those traits. When you search for passages about patience, you eventually come to James 5:11, which speaks of the "patience of Job" (KJV). Sometimes a topical Bible contains in its listings the examples of persons who demonstrate the topic it is presenting.

You can use a study of the life of Barnabas to develop the capacity for encouragement in your life. To begin the study, you should define encouragement as including stimulation, consolation, cheering, or exhorting someone. The *King James Version* describes Barnabas as "the son of consolation" (Acts 4:36), and the *New American Standard Bible* translates the same verse as "Son of Encouragement." Depending on the Bible version you use, you can use a concordance to study either the word *consolation* or the word *encouragement*.

Because Barnabas is clearly a person who gave encouragement to others, you could study his life to learn about encouraging other Christians. You will find references to some of his actions in Acts 4:36; 9:27; and 11:23-26. You will also find several references to the actions of Barnabas on the first missionary journey of Paul in Acts 13—14. After Paul and Barnabas separated, Barnabas spent time with John Mark (see Acts 15:36-39).

To use a Bible personality to do a character-trait study, use the same steps you used yesterday. However, you should limit your consideration to references to that trait in the life of that character. When you have located and listed references to the trait in the person's life, use the following reflection questions to help you identify ways to apply what you learned about the trait to your relationship with God, to your own life, to your relationships with others, and to the church.

- What in this person's life demonstrates the character trait I am studying?
- How did this character trait affect others?
- What final result did this character trait produce in this person's life and in the lives of others?

---

† Use Acts 4:36; 9:27; 11:23-26; 13—14; 15:36-39 to do a **study of the trait of encouragement in the life of Barnabas. Use the worksheet "Character-Trait Bible Study" on pages 139-140.**

Character-Trait Bible Study

Trait: _____

Dictionary definition: _____

_____

Synonyms: _____

Antonyms: _____

Bible definition and teachings: _____

_____

Summary of Bible teachings: _____

_____

Reflections:

• What are some benefits of this trait in my life and in the lives of others?

_____

_____

• What are some problems this trait could produce in my life or in the lives of others?

_____

_____

• Is there a promise or warning from God about this trait? If so, what is it?

_____

• What factors produce this trait? _____

_____

• What effect does this trait produce in the life of the church?

_____

_____

• Is this trait a part of God's character? ❑ Yes ❑ No

Ways to apply the study—

• to my relationship with God: _____

_____

• to my own life: _____

_____

• to my relationships with others: _____

_____

• to the church: _____

_____

By studying these passages, you should have been able to summarize what they teach about encouragement. Then you should have been able to apply these teachings to the four areas you have studied.

Tomorrow you will learn the final method in your two-week study of ways to apply the Bible.

———

Answers to Bible character exercise: 1. g, 2. e, 3. b, 4. l, 5. a, 6. d, 7. i, 8. c, 9. k, 10. f, 11. j, 12. h.

Day 3
Purposes and Principles of Devotional Bible Study

You have learned two different methods of Bible study to apply the Bible to your relationship with God, to your own life, to your relationships with others, and to the church.

† **Name the two types of study you have learned for applying the Bible.**

1. _____

2. _____

You have examined and practiced biographical and character-trait Bible study. Today you will begin learning how to do devotional Bible study and apply it to the four areas. This method of Bible study emphasizes the use of the Bible to change your life. Bible study can become dead and lifeless unless you apply what you learn. The devotional method of Bible study encourages you to make meaningful application of what you study.

When you studied the analytical method of Bible study in week 4, the importance of observing facts and truths in the Bible was emphasized, as well as the importance of applying the Bible to your life. In devotional Bible study the primary emphasis is on the application of the Bible. You still have an interest in the facts and truths of a passage of Scripture, but your primary emphasis is on ways the passage can change your life. This method depends on a spirit of eagerness to do God's will and to let God's message change your life.

Here is the process you will follow for devotional Bible study.

1. *Always begin with exactly what the passage means.* If you don't understand what a passage is saying, your application can be wrong.

✝ Read Ephesians 4:26. Write what the verse means.

_____

_____

Turn to week 2, day 1 (page 34) and recall the actual meaning Paul intended for this verse to convey.

In Ephesians 4:26 Paul was not urging us to show anger based on petty feelings or wounded pride. Paul knew that righteous anger exists. He also knew that this kind of anger can quickly change into anger that is selfish and uncontrolled. Paul was warning us against letting our righteous anger get out of control. Application of a passage must rely on correct interpretation of its meaning.

2. *Evaluate the kind of passage you are trying to apply.* You must know whether a passage is talking about a truth that is timeless or temporary. Timeless truth applies to people of any time or circumstance. Temporary truth applies only to a specific individual or group at a specific point in history.

✝ Read the following verses and indicate for each whether its truth is timeless or temporary.

Leviticus 11:1-7 ❑ Timeless ❑ Temporary

Luke 20:25 ❑ Timeless ❑ Temporary

The application of some Old Testament verses is affected by information from the New Testament. The food restrictions of Leviticus 11 may contain helpful health information about eating. However, in Mark 7:19 Jesus declared that following those laws is not necessary in our spiritual lives. Some Bible passages, like Luke 20:25, describe a condition we may not face today. However, the principle that was used in the Bible to face the condition in the first century may still be valid today. For example, we are not ruled by Caesar today, but God expects us to give both to the government and to God.

3. *Relate the passage to others on the same subject.* This increases your understanding of the meaning of the passage you are studying. Read Matthew 7:7. Jesus' teachings on prayer suggest that those who keep on asking can expect God to answer their prayers.

✝ **Read James 4:3 and 1 John 5:14-15. Summarize the ways they change the way you would apply Matthew 7:7.**

James 4:3: _____

_____

1 John 5:14-15: _____

_____

Such passages as James 4:3 and 1 John 5:14-15 give other factors to consider in seeking answers to prayer. You will want to modify your understanding of Matthew 7:7 in light of such passages' teachings.

4. *Determine ways the passage can be applied.* A passage can be applied in many ways. You may learn a truth about God that you can apply to the political, economic, or social arena. You may find a truth about yourself that can give you a higher call of commitment to God's will. You may discover insights that will change your attitudes toward and relationships with coworkers, neighbors, and even enemies. You may learn goals and challenges you can pray into reality in your church.

Doing a Devotional Bible Study

1. Always begin with exactly what the passage means.
2. Evaluate the kind of passage you are trying to apply.
3. Relate the passage to others on the same subject.
4. Determine ways the passage can be applied.

✝ Begin a devotional study of Ephesians 4:32, a verse you memorized in week 1, following steps 1–3 above. You will add step 4 tomorrow. Complete the worksheet "Devotional Bible Study" on page 145 to record your responses. (A master copy of this worksheet can be found on page 221.)

Tomorrow we will help you evaluate this assignment and complete your devotional study by identifying ways to apply Ephesians 4:32.

✝ You should have memorized this week's Scripture-memory verses by now. Write the passage from memory.

_____

_____

_____

_____

_____

Devotional Bible Study

Scripture reference: _____

Summary of the passage's meaning/teaching:

_____

_____

_____

_____

_____

_____

Is the teaching timeless or temporary? ❑ Timeless   ❑ Temporary

Related Scripture references and their teachings:

_____

_____

_____

_____

_____

Day 4
Applying a Devotional Bible Study

Yesterday you completed a devotional Bible study of Ephesians 4:32, except for the final and very important step of applying the verse to life.

✝ **Can you identify the four areas to which you will apply devotional Bible study? Name them.**

1. _____

2. _____

3. _____

4. _____

At this session you will complete your devotional Bible study of Ephesians 4:32 by identifying ways to apply it to your relationship with God, to your own life, to your relationships with others, and to the church. But first let's process the way you completed your worksheet yesterday.

First, you recognized that you can use devotional Bible study as a part of your daily system of Bible reading. You can also use it to make a specific passage of Scripture come alive in your personal experience. When you do devotional Bible study, you should continually ask yourself, *How can I use this Bible truth in my life?*

There is no single way to write a summary or the main teaching of Ephesians 4:32. An interesting fact about devotional Bible study is that the summary of the passage and its teachings will reflect the needs a person feels most deeply. We don't know what you wrote on your worksheet, but you probably dealt with questions like these.

- What happens if the person or persons I think I need to forgive do not want my forgiveness?
- Is my forgiving another person the same as God's forgiving that person?

- Does forgiving a person mean that I act as if that person had never wronged me?

Next, what did you decide about the timeliness of the passage? Is its truth temporary or timeless? The teaching in this passage is a timeless truth. This passage contains a truth that God intends for us to apply fully today.

The next step in your study was to identify related passages that you could compare with the passage you were studying. Some of the more prominent New Testament passages that deal with forgiveness are Matthew 5:23-24; 18:15; Luke 23:34; Acts 7:60; and Colossians 3:13.

Now let's complete the study by finding ways you can apply this passage. Follow these steps to apply devotional Bible study.

1. *Pray that God will give you insight about the application of the passage.*
2. *Meditate on the passage.* As you meditate, try to imagine how you might apply the passage. In the case of Ephesians 4:32, consider someone you need to forgive. What attitude must you overcome to offer forgiveness? How can you express forgiveness? In person? By a telephone call? Via email? With a letter? What can you do to demonstrate that your forgiveness is genuine? Let me suggest a simple device you can use to direct your meditation. As you meditate, ask yourself five questions, which form the acrostic PEACE. As you pray, ask yourself:

   Is there any—
   Promise to claim or praise to offer God?
   Example to follow or avoid?
   Action or attitude to change?
   Command to obey?
   Error to avoid?
3. *Write specific, practical ways the passage can be applied.* Think of specific and practical ways to apply the passage to your relationship with God, to your own life, to your relationships with others, and to the church. Merely saying, "I will be more forgiving" is not specific enough. Offering to express forgiveness to everyone who has ever sinned against you is not practical.
4. *Memorize the verse or verses you have studied.* Because you memorized Ephesians 4:32 in week 1, this verse is now a

tool God can continually use to help you in the process of forgiving others. The challenge of forgiveness requires time for mastery, and continual help is essential.

5. *Put the application into practice.* In the matter of forgiveness you may need to visit someone, make a phone call, or write a letter to express forgiveness to someone who may have harmed or injured you. Avoid saying to someone, "If I've done anything wrong, I want to apologize." Specifically mention the incident that demands forgiveness. Also, it is best if you admit negative thoughts about a person only to God. Mentioning them to the other person will cause him to wonder what you are thinking.

Five Steps to Apply a Devotional Bible Study

1. Pray that God will give you insight about the application of the passage.
2. Meditate on the passage.
3. Write specific, practical ways the passage can be applied.
4. Memorize the verse or verses you have studied.
5. Put the application into practice.

✝ Complete the worksheet "Applying Devotional Bible Study" on page 149. (A master copy of this worksheet can be found on page 222.) Make your application of Ephesians 4:32 by following the steps you studied today. Be sure to allow adequate time for the meditation process, using the PEACE acrostic, and for writing applications to the four areas of your life.

Applying Devotional Bible Study

Scripture reference: _____

1. Pray that God will give you insight about the application of the passage.

2. Meditate on the passage, asking yourself:

Is there any—
❑ Promise to claim or praise to offer God?
❑ Example to follow or avoid?
❑ Action or attitude to change?
❑ Command to obey?
❑ Error to avoid?

3. Ways this passage can be applied—

• to your relationship with God: _____

_____

• to your own life: _____

_____

• to your relationships with others: _____

_____

• to the church: _____

_____

4. Memorize the verse(s).

5. Ways you can put the application into practice: _____

_____

Day 5
Practicing a Devotional Bible Study

Today you will spend all of your time completing two devotional Bible studies. This practice will be important in honing the skills you need to apply God's Word in life-changing ways.

✝ Complete devotional Bible studies of Lamentations 3:22-23 and 1 Peter 4:19. Use the worksheets "Devotional Bible Study" on pages 151 and 153 and "Applying Devotional Bible Study" on pages 152 and 154. Try to complete these studies on your own. Consult the chart on pages 155-156 only if you get bogged down.

After your intensive, detailed examination of these two Scripture passages, take a moment to recapture a broad view of what you have been studying over the past two weeks.

✝ Name the three Bible-study methods you have learned to help you apply the Bible to your life.

1. _____

2. _____

3. _____

Record the four areas of life in which you learned to apply Bible study.

1. _____

2. _____

3. _____

4. _____

Devotional Bible Study

Scripture reference: _____

Summary of the passage's meaning/teaching:

_____

_____

_____

_____

_____

_____

Is the teaching timeless or temporary? ❑ Timeless ❑ Temporary

Related Scripture references and their teachings:

_____

_____

_____

_____

_____

_____

Applying Devotional Bible Study

Scripture reference: _____

1. Pray that God will give you insight about the application of the passage.

2. Meditate on the passage, asking yourself:

Is there any—
❑ **Promise** to claim or praise to offer God?
❑ **Example** to follow or avoid?
❑ **Action** or attitude to change?
❑ **Command** to obey?
❑ **Error** to avoid?

3. Ways this passage can be applied—

• to your relationship with God: _____

_____

• to your own life: _____

_____

• to your relationships with others: _____

_____

• to the church: _____

_____

4. Memorize the verse(s).

5. Ways you can put the application into practice: _____

_____

Devotional Bible Study

Scripture reference: _____

Summary of the passage's meaning/teaching:

_____

_____

_____

_____

_____

_____

Is the teaching timeless or temporary? ❑ Timeless   ❑ Temporary

Related Scripture references and their teachings:

_____

_____

_____

_____

_____

_____

Applying Devotional Bible Study

Scripture reference: _____

1. Pray that God will give you insight about the application of the passage.

2. Meditate on the passage, asking yourself:

Is there any—
❏ **P**romise to claim or praise to offer God?
❏ **E**xample to follow or avoid?
❏ **A**ction or attitude to change?
❏ **C**ommand to obey?
❏ **E**rror to avoid?

3. Ways this passage can be applied—

• to your relationship with God: _____

_____

• to your own life: _____

_____

• to your relationships with others: _____

_____

• to the church: _____

_____

4. Memorize the verse(s).

5. Ways you can put the application into practice: _____

_____

	Lamentations 3:22-23
Summary	Read Lamentations 3:22-23 and summarize the meaning of the passage. Do a background study of this passage to learn such facts as who wrote it, when it was written, and how the writer came to speak as he did in these verses. A Bible commentary can help.
Timeless or Temporary?	Evaluate this passage for its present application. Because the writer is stating a truth about God, we can recognize that its content was true for the writer and is true for us.
Related Scripture	Can you find other passages that teach a similar truth about God? You might investigate Psalm 84:11; 118:24; Romans 8:28-31.
Application	As you apply this passage to your own life, can you think of specific subjects you often think about instead of God's mercies? Do these subjects cause you worry, fear, resentment, or depression? How could it help your problem if you reflected more on what God will do for you in His faithfulness and mercy? Which words of the PEACE acrostic are most useful to you here? Do you find a promise, example, action or attitude, command, or error you must observe? Can you find a specific application of this verse to your life? In what area of your life is it helpful? Does it change your idea of God, your understanding of yourself, your relationship to another person, or your attitude toward your church?

	1 Peter 4:19
Summary	Read 1 Peter 4:19 and summarize the meaning of the passage. As you do so, consider the type of suffering Peter was describing. Was it suffering for your faith, or was it the trials of life such as sickness, general discouragement, or the loss of a job? Can the principles Peter mentions apply to both of these situations? Also ask yourself: What does it mean to suffer according to God's will? In what ways is God faithful? How has He shown this to me?
Timeless or Temporary?	Although Peter addressed a specific situation involving suffering and a specific audience in Asia Minor around A.D. 62 to 69, the teaching of this verse has universal application to believers today who suffer.
Related Scripture	Compare this passage with others that teach the same truth. Among those are Psalm 73; 2 Corinthians 4:16-18; James 1:2-5. Can you add others?
Application	As you apply this passage to your own life, can you think of specific situations that are causing you suffering? Can you visualize what might be involved in trusting yourself to God in this matter? Which of the words of the PEACE acrostic are most applicable to you? Does this verse provide a promise, example, action or attitude, command, or error to be noted? Can you write a specific application of this verse? What is the primary area of application you are making? Does it deal with your understanding of God, your understanding of yourself, your relationship with someone else, or your relationship with your church? Here are some considerations to assist you in applying this passage. Most people respond to difficulty in life by showing self-pity, by becoming angry at God or someone else, or by losing all will to endure. Have you shown any of these responses? Recognize that all of us encounter daily hardships and difficulties in which we must have God's strength and presence. Don't respond to this passage by saying, "If I ever need this truth, I'll remember it." You already need God's strength and must apply it daily.

You have now completed a two-week study of biographical, character-trait, and devotional Bible study. No matter which method you use to apply the Bible, you may apply its teachings to your relationship with God, to your own life, to your relationships with others, and to the church.

We hope these studies have been rewarding. Applying the truths of God's Word to your life should be the end result of all Bible study. That is a significant way you grow to be more like your Master Teacher, Jesus Christ.

✝ Write from memory your Scripture-memory verses for this week.

_____

_____

_____

_____

If you have time, complete a devotional study of these verses. If not, write one way you can apply these verses, perhaps by sharing them with someone who is undergoing hardship.

_____

_____

Review the previous weeks' Scripture-memory verses.

✝ Close this week's study in prayer. Seek God's guidance as you apply His Word to your life. Be specific in your request using the points of application you identified over the past two weeks.

Week 8

Keys to Understanding the Bible: Word Study, Images, and Grammar

Day 1
How to Complete a Word Study

Day 2
Practicing a Word Study

Day 3
Understanding Biblical Images: Comparison, Association, and Personification

Day 4
Understanding Biblical Images: Understatement, Overstatement, Irony, and Rhetorical Questions

Day 5
Understanding the Grammar of the Bible

Scripture-Memory Verse
May the God of peace Himself sanctify you entirely; and may your spirit and soul and body be preserved complete, without blame at the coming of our Lord Jesus Christ.
1 Thessalonians 5:23

For the past several weeks you have learned Bible-study methods that allow you to interpret the Bible accurately and apply it meaningfully. For the remainder of your study you will take a narrower look at specific tools for Bible study that will help you discover even more about the Bible and that will enrich your time in the Word. Over the next two weeks you will focus on the following keys to understanding the Bible.

1. Word study
2. Biblical images
3. The grammar of the Bible
4. Topical Bible study
5. Doctrinal Bible study

Day 1
How to Complete a Word Study

We will begin by learning how to complete a word study. The Bible most of us use is easy to read and understand. Many good English translations and paraphrases are available to us. The authors of the Bible did not write in English but in Hebrew, Aramaic, and Greek. Because the words of these languages do not always have exact equivalents in English, a knowledge of the original languages is a great help in studying the Bible. Most of us, however, are not scholars. We must use our English Bible and the aids for Bible study that are available to us. Word studies allow us to discover the original meanings of the words that appear in our English Bible.

Completing a Word Study

1. Select the word to study.
2. Define the word.
3. Discover Bible usages of the word.
4. Define the Bible meaning.
5. Summarize what you have learned about the word.
6. Plan applications.

You will use a six-step procedure for completing a word study.
1. *Select the word to study.* Until you have developed your skills in doing a word study, you should not select a word with a broad meaning. Select a word with a meaning narrow enough to study easily. A narrow word is a word that has a rather limited meaning and usage. In contrast, a broad word deals with a theme of the Bible that is large and prominent.
2. *Define the word.* Look up and record the definition from an English dictionary; include synonyms and antonyms.

✝ **Imagine you are doing a study of *sanctification*. What is the dictionary definition? Summarize it below.**

_____

_____

_____

List synonyms for sanctification.

_____

_____

List antonyms for sanctification.

_____

_____

3. *Discover Bible usages of the word.* A concordance is a valuable tool for completing word studies. This resource lists Bible words and gives references to their usages. Find and list Bible passages where the word is used.

✝ **Find the word *sanctification* in a concordance. Record in the margin references of passages in which the word is used.**

Part of this step is discovering the meaning of the word as it is used in the Bible. You do not have to be a scholar to do this. A Bible dictionary or a good reference Bible will help you understand Bible words. Some study Bibles contain an encyclopedia that explains many Bible words.

✝ **Use a Bible dictionary or a study Bible to discover meanings of the word *sanctification* or *sanctify*. Write a couple of these below.**

_____

_____

You probably discovered that the word is used in both the Old Testament and New Testament and that the English words *consecrate, holy,* and *holiness* are sometimes used to translate the words that are usually translated *sanctification*. These words mean *set apart* or *separated to God*.

✝ **Using a concordance, write in the margin references of the verses in which the words *consecrate, holy,* or *holiness* appear.**

Modern English versions give additional information about the meanings or shades of meaning the word may have.

✝ **The word *holiness* appears in Romans 6:19 in the *King James Version*. Use at least two modern English translations and write below words that are used instead of *holiness*.**

_____

You will also want to make notes about the contexts in which these words are used. Observe the books in which the words appear, the writers who use the words, and the usages of the words in the texts where they appear.

† Write three of the references you found for *sanctification, sanctify, consecrate, holy,* or *holiness* and your comments about how the words are used.

- _____
_____

- _____
_____

- _____
_____

Comments you might make about each verse include the motivation toward sanctification, the means of obtaining sanctification, and what is included in sanctification.

4. *Define the Bible meaning.* Write a definition that expresses the way the word is used in the Bible.

† Based on what you have discovered, how would you define sanctification as it is used in the Bible?

_____

_____

_____

Looking up a word in *Strong's Exhaustive Concordance* is an excellent way to determine its Bible meaning. This concordance not only lists references to verses in which the word is used but also cross-references the word to a dictionary that gives meanings from the original language in which the word was written.

✝ Check the definition you wrote against the one found in a concordance.

5. *Summarize what you have learned about the word.* The summary may be an outline of biblical teachings about the word, or it may be an original paragraph that you compose. Your summary is important because it opens the door for the applications you will plan in the next step.

✝ Summarize what you have learned from your word study of sanctification. Use the margin if you need more space.

_____

_____

6. *Plan applications.* Write ways you can apply your word study to your relationship with God, to your own life, to your relationships with others, and to the church.

✝ See if you can apply your study of *sanctification* to—

your relationship with God: _____

_____

your own life: _____

_____

your relationships with others: _____

_____

the church: _____

_____

By this time you should have developed a reasonable degree of skill in identifying and planning these applications. In the next session you will have an opportunity to practice a word study.

✝ Your Scripture-memory verse for this week is 1 Thessalonians 5:23. Use the Scripture-memory card at the center of your workbook to begin learning this verse.

Day 2
Practicing a Word Study

Yesterday you were introduced to six steps for completing a word study. Today you will have an opportunity to practice.

1. *Select the word to study.* Decide on the Bible word you want to study. For the purpose of practice, we will do this step for you by assigning you the word *anxious*. This study will be spiritually helpful, and the word is narrow enough that you can follow it easily.

✝ Duplicate and examine the worksheet "Word Study" on pages 164-165. Write the word *anxious* at the top. Complete on your copy the remaining sections of the worksheet on your own before reading further. Refer to yesterday's lesson if you need to review the steps to follow.

Word Study

Word: _____

Dictionary definition: _____

_____

_____

Synonyms:_____

Antonyms:_____

Bible usages: _____

_____

_____

_____

_____

Bible meaning: _____

_____

_____

_____

Summary: _____

_____

_____

_____

_____

Ways to apply the study—

• to your relationship with God: _____

_____

• to your own life: _____

_____

• to your relationships with others: _____

_____

• to the church: _____

_____

Let's look at your work one step at a time. Your work does not have to match ours; your work will reflect your own spiritual walk.

2. *Define the word.* A good dictionary made it easy to list synonyms, but our dictionary did not suggest any antonyms. However, examining the synonyms gave us clues about the antonyms. How does our list compare with yours?

Synonyms	Antonyms
Care	Assurance
Insecurity	Certainty
Worry	Confidence
Concern	Trust

3. *Discover Bible usages of the word.* If you were working with the *King James Version*, you might have been surprised to discover that the word anxious does not appear. What did you do then? We started checking out the synonyms and discovered several passages related to *care* and *carefulness*. That got us started. Were you able to work with a Bible dictionary or a concordance such as *Strong's Exhaustive Concordance*? If so, did you discover several meanings for *care* and *carefulness*? You should have discovered that some care is not worry but is interest and goodwill. You probably got an indication of this when working with the dictionary definition. We trust that you confined your search in the concordance to words that show a kind of care that causes worry, fret, or anxiety. We are using the *New American Standard Bible* as our basic text for this study. Did you look up the words *anxious, care,* and *worry* in the concordance of your *New American Standard Bible*? Check your findings against ours.

- Verses that use the word *anxious*:

Matthew 6:25	Matthew 6:34	Luke 12:26
Matthew 6:27	Matthew 10:19	Philippians 4:6
Matthew 6:31	Mark 13:11	

- Verses that use the word *care*:

Genesis 50:24	Ezekiel 34:12	1 Corinthians 12:25
Psalms 8:4	Mark 4:38	1 Timothy 3:5
Psalms 142:4	Luke 10:34	1 Peter 5:7

• Verses that use the word *worry*:
Luke 8:14   Luke 10:41   Luke 12:29

We hope that as you studied the various passages, you made careful notes about who was using the word and the books in which it is used. Failing to do this as a part of your study is taking a dangerous shortcut. Another dangerous shortcut is not taking time to study the same passage in modern-English translations. It helped us see how other translations used words like *being bothered* or *fretting*.

✝ **Record in the margin one word or phrase you found that was helpful or interesting to you.**

4. *Define the Bible meaning.* As you studied these verses, you probably noticed that some of them refer to being concerned in a legitimate way. Care and concern are not always wrong.

✝ **Arrange the verses from step 3 in the two categories in the following chart.**

Legitimate Concern   **Harmful Anxiety**

_____   _____

_____   _____

_____   _____

_____   _____

_____   _____

_____   _____

_____   _____

_____   _____

_____   _____

5. *Summarize what you have learned about the word.* The way you wrote your summary is not important. However, it is important that you identified relevant teachings.
   • How concerned should you be about things?
   • What attitude should you have about the future?
   • What attitude should you have about life's nonessentials?
   • What should your attitude be about life in this world?
   • What does the Bible teach about trying to please the wrong people?

   We hope you were careful to note that in some cases a certain amount of care is healthy and productive. In other cases, care is wrong.

✝ **What cure for care is suggested in 1 Peter 5:7?**

_____

That cure should be an important part of your summary.

6. *Plan applications.* Application is the step that determines whether your Bible study will be academic or life-transforming. Even though this assignment was a practice exercise, we hope you were serious enough to pray about the applications you identified and to commit yourself to them.

Word study is an informative method of Bible study. This method focuses intensively on the small details of word meanings. To get the most from word study, combine it with other study methods you have learned, such as the synthetic or historical method, so that you can get a full picture of what God is saying. Tomorrow you will learn a second key to understanding the Bible.

Day 3
Understanding Biblical Images:
Comparison, Association, and Personification

Sometimes the truths of the Bible are so profound that they cannot be expressed with normal word associations. Often figures of speech are used in the Bible to express these truths. Figures of speech present pictures and images to express deep, difficult ideas in a vivid, memorable manner. Understanding the way figures of speech are used in the Bible can help you better interpret what the Bible is saying when it uses these images.

Figures of speech are normally taken from the background of the speaker or writer who uses them. Generally, they are easily understood by both the writer and the hearer or reader. When Paul referred to himself and Timothy as bondservants of Christ Jesus, he was using a metaphor based on the practice of slavery in the New Testament world. Studying the figures of speech in the Bible often increases your understanding of the culture, background, and history of Bible times.

Figures of speech in the Bible appear in different forms. Over the next two days you will examine these figures of speech:

❑ Simile   ❑ Personification   ❑ Oxymoron
❑ Metaphor   ❑ Euphemism   ❑ Irony
❑ Metonymy   ❑ Meiosis   ❑ Rhetorical question
❑ Synecdoche   ❑ Hyperbole

✝ In the preceding list, check the figures of speech you are familiar with.

Common Biblical Images

Simile	Personification	Oxymoron
Metaphor	Euphemism	Irony
Metonymy	Meiosis	Rhetorical question
Synecdoche	Hyperbole	

The most common images in the Bible compare two objects. A **simile** (SIM-uh-le) is a figure of speech that uses such words as *like* or *as* in comparing two unrelated objects. A metaphor (MET-uh-for) also compares two unrelated objects without using the terms *like* or *as*. Rather, a metaphor compares the two objects by suggesting that one is the other.

Let's look at some similes in the Bible and observe how they help you picture more vividly the idea the writer is trying to communicate. First, form the mental picture of a violent sea storm. Picture one wave being driven and tossed by the wind. Concentrate on that wave.

†What feelings do you have when you think about the storm-tossed wave? What descriptive words and phrases come to mind? Write those descriptive words and phrases on and around the wave in the drawing.

✝ Now read James 1:6. Observe how the simile makes the writer's words spring to life before your very eyes! While the feelings and mental images are still fresh, write a brief description of a person torn by indecision.

_____

_____

Now imagine that you are looking at yourself in a mirror. Concentrate on what you see in the mirror. Visualize your face, your hair, the line of your chin. How are you dressed? Now imagine that you have walked away from the mirror and suddenly you cannot remember what you saw when you looked at yourself. No matter how hard you try, you cannot remember.

✝ What conclusions can you draw about yourself? What kind of person cannot remember his own reflection in a mirror? Read James 1:23-24. What was James saying about a person who hears God's Word and then does not obey it?

_____

_____

Do you see how a simile communicates a dimension of meaning that would otherwise be difficult to convey?

A metaphor suggests a comparison by stating that one object is another object. Jesus used a metaphor when He stated that His followers are " 'the salt of the earth' " and " 'the light of the world' " (Matthew 5:13-14).

✝ Read these verses. Complete the metaphors James used.

James 3:6: The tongue is a _____.

James 4:14: You are a _____.

James used metaphors when he compared the tongue to a fire and when he related earthly life to a temporary vapor that vanishes. Think about these metaphors. Catch the vividness they bring to what James was trying to communicate.

Another figure of speech involves the use of association. In **metonymy** (muh-TON-uh-me) the name of one thing is used for another thing because a cause may suggest an effect or an effect may describe a cause. In Luke 16:29 Jesus used the term "Moses and the prophets" to describe the writings of which they were the authors. Moses and the prophets could speak through these writings to warn the brothers of the rich fool to avoid the torment he was experiencing.

Another figure of speech that uses association is **synecdoche** (suh-NEK-duh-ke). Here a part is used for a whole, or a whole is used for a part. In Acts 27:37 (KJV) the term *souls* is used to designate the whole person. In Micah 4:3 the abandonment of two weapons, swords and spears, stands for total disarmament.

Another figure of speech the Bible uses is **personification**. This means something that has no life is treated as if it had life.

✝ Read Matthew 6:34. Identify the personification Jesus used and explain the idea He was trying to communicate.

_____

_____

When Jesus said that " 'tomorrow will care for itself,' " He was viewing tomorrow as a living person surrounded with care.

The Psalms often personify the various parts of nature. The psalmist did this in Psalm 114:5-6 when he asked:

What ails you, O sea, that you flee?
O Jordan, that you turn back?
O mountains, that you skip like rams?
O hills, like lambs?

Here the sea and mountains, which have no life, appear as living beings. James used personification in James 5:4 when he said that "the pay of the laborers who mowed your fields, and which has been withheld by you, cries out against you."

Personification expresses the deep feeling and imagination of religious language. Interpreting the meanings of these passages is not difficult. The writer does not actually see the quality, thing, or idea as alive, but he uses symbolic language that adds vividness and power to communication.

Today you have seen ways the images used in the Bible add rich dimensions of meaning to your Bible study. Figures of speech also add beauty and vivid expression to the language of the Bible. When you study figures of speech, your imagination and senses are stimulated so that you can fully enjoy the splendor of God's written Word.

✝ Write from memory this week's Scripture-memory verse.

_____

_____

_____

Day 4
Understanding Biblical Images: Understatement, Overstatement, Irony, and Rhetorical Questions

Yesterday you examined the way several types of figures of speech are used in the Bible to convey the writers' meaning.

✝ Recall the two images of comparison you studied:

S _____ and M _____

What are the two images of association you studied:

M _____ and S _____

Name the fifth figure of speech you studied:

P _____

Yesterday you examined two images of comparison, simile and metaphor; two images of association, metonymy and synecdoche; and personification. Today you will learn about other figures of speech that are used in the Bible.

Another type of image that frequently appears in the Bible is understatement. Sometimes understatement is used to avoid a blunt or distasteful tone in the writing. This biblical image is called **euphemism** (YOU-fuh-mizem). We use euphemism in English when we say that someone has passed away instead of bluntly saying that the person has died.

† **Read Acts 1:25 and identify the euphemism used.**

_____

Identify the euphemism in 1 Thessalonians 4:14.

_____

When Peter urged the church to choose a replacement for Judas, he described Judas as one who had " 'turned aside to go to his own place.' " His understatement allowed him to refer to the final destiny of Judas without any harsh, threatening suggestion. In 1 Thessalonians 4:14 Paul used euphemism when he described some deceased Thessalonian Christians as "those who have fallen asleep in Jesus." In death these Christians looked as if they were asleep, but in truth they were with Jesus.

Another type of understatement is **meiosis** (my-O-sis). This use of understatement calls attention to a comment or an idea by using a negative statement to declare a positive truth.

† **Identify the meiosis in the following passages and state what the writer is actually saying.**

Galatians 5:22-23: _____

_____

1 Thessalonians 2:15: _____

_____

In Galatians 5:22-23 Paul listed the fruit of the Spirit, a collection of godly character traits the Holy Spirit can produce in a Christian's life. Paul concluded, "Against such things there is no law." This deliberate understatement emphasizes that no law-enforcement agency would need to protect its citizens against love, joy, peace, and self-control. Paul's understatement calls attention to the godly influence of the fruit of the Spirit.

In 1 Thessalonians 2:15 Paul described the Jews as people who killed the Lord Jesus and the prophets and drove away Christian preachers who attempted to declare the truth. Then he added, "They are not pleasing to God." By deliberate understatement he called attention to just how much the Jews displeased God.

To determine the presence of understatement, concentrate and reflect on what the Bible is actually saying. Wherever a statement or comment is so obviously true that it doesn't need to be stated, the Bible writers practiced understatement for effect and emphasis.

Another type of figure of speech is overstatement. One form of overstatement is known as **hyperbole** (hi-PUR-buh-le). This is an intentional overstatement for emphasis and communication. Paul used hyperbole when he said that the gospel had gone into "all the world" (Colossians 1:6). The Christian message had not gone into every geographic corner of the world. But, it had spread over the inhabited world. No one would accuse Paul of error. He chose hyperbole to dramatically describe the spread of Christianity.

☦ Read Matthew 5:30. Identify the hyperbole Jesus used.

_____

In this verse Jesus used hyperbole when He said, " 'If your right hand makes you stumble, cut it off, and throw it from you.' " No one should literally remove his right hand. However, he must show the same zeal in fighting sin that he might show by removing the hand.

John used hyperbole when he said that if all of the events of Jesus' life were written down, "even the world itself would not contain the books which were written" (John 21:25). John used hyperbole to emphasize that Jesus' deeds were much more numerous than he had written.

Another figure of speech that involves overstatement is called the **oxymoron** (ox-i-MOR-on). This is a figure of speech in which opposite or contradictory ideas appear. We use this figure of speech in English when we speak of a thunderous silence. The union of these opposing ideas can have an arresting effect on readers. Paul used this image when he described the Macedonian Christians as people whose "deep poverty overflowed in the wealth of their liberality" (2 Corinthians 8:2).

✝ **What do you think Paul meant by combining poverty and generosity in this sentence?**

Poverty doesn't normally lead to generosity. When Paul combined the two ideas, he expressed a gripping thought that claims our attention.

The Bible also uses **irony**. This is a figure of speech when the words suggest the opposite of the writer's true intent. If you jump into icy water, someone may ask you, "How's the water?" You may answer, "Fine!" through clenched, chattering teeth, meaning the very opposite of what you say. This is irony.

✝ **Read the Roman soldiers' words in Matthew 27:29. What do you think the soldiers wanted to communicate?**

The Roman soldiers used irony when they welcomed Jesus with the words " 'Hail, King of the Jews!' " (Matthew 27:29). The

Jews actually felt scorn and contempt, although their words showed a pretended form of worship.

Sometimes a Bible writer asks a question for effect and purpose. Because the answer is obvious, the question simply becomes the means of directing the reader's thought toward a central idea. Paul used this figure of speech in Romans 6:1 when he said: "What shall we say then? Are we to continue in sin that grace might increase?" Paul quickly answered his question with the words "May it never be!" The answer to the question was already clear. He used the question to draw the reader's attention to an idea. This is known as a **rhetorical question**.

This concludes your study of many figures of speech Bible writers used to communicate their ideas more vividly.

✝ **Review biblical figures of speech by matching each figure of speech on the left with the correct definition on the right.**

___ 1. synecdoche	a. Comparing one object to another using like or as
___ 2. rhetorical question	b. Comparing one object to another without using like or as
___ 3. irony	c. Using the name of one person/object to represent another person/object
___ 4. metaphor	d. Using a part to represent the whole or vice versa
___ 5. euphemism	e. Speaking of an inanimate object as if it had life
___ 6. meiosis	f. Using understatement to soften a statement's blunt or distasteful nature
___ 7. simile	g. Using a negative statement to declare a positive truth
___ 8. oxymoron	h. Using exaggeration or overstatement
___ 9. personification	i. Exaggerating or overstating the opposite idea from the truth being stated
___ 10. hyperbole	j. Using a statement that expresses the opposite of the actual feeling
___ 11. metonymy	k. Asking a question for which the answer is obvious

That was a lot to learn in two days, so you may need to go back and review if you missed any. The correct answers are: 1. d, 2. k, 3. j, 4. b, 5. f, 6. g, 7. a, 8. i, 9. e, 10. h, 11. c.

Understanding figures of speech can greatly enhance your understanding of the Bible. They make the reading of the Bible more vivid and interesting. Biblical writers used them to teach the truth and oppose error. Learning to recognize and appreciate these figures of speech can help you become more effective in your own presentation of God's message.

Day 5
Understanding the Grammar of the Bible

One important key to understanding the Bible is a knowledge of grammar. Like the other keys you have studied, grammatical study has a narrow focus. It is not something you will do by itself. Instead, you can use it to add depths of meaning to other types of Bible study such as synthetic and analytical study.

Grammatical Forms of Statements in the Bible

1. Statement of fact
2. Warning
3. Promise
4. Command

Let's begin by considering the four grammatical **forms of statements** encountered in the Bible. Each type of statement has characteristics that suggests how it should be interpreted.

1. *Statement of fact.* This form of statement appears in books that deal with historical matters such as 1 and 2 Samuel and Acts. It also appears in the epistles of Paul, Peter, and John. In Philippians 1:21 Paul stated, "To me, to live is Christ, and to die is gain." Paul was stating his view of life's most important priority.

† Why do you think it is important to recognize statements of fact in the Bible?

_____

_____

It is important to recognize statements of fact for what they are so that you will not read other meanings into them. Some early Christians tried to see a symbol of Jesus' victory on the cross in the number 318 in Genesis 14:14. The Bible is not using that number to point to Jesus. It is merely saying that Abraham took 318 men to fight.

2. *Warning.* A warning is an alarm or a signal to avoid something. The Bible frequently introduces the warning with the words *beware* or *take heed.* When you see warnings, you know that these statements contain advice you must apply. The Book of Hebrews, which contains many warnings, expresses one with the words "Take heed, ... lest there be in any of you an evil heart of unbelief, in departing from the living God" (Hebrews 3:12, KJV).

✝ **Read Matthew 7:15. How did Jesus use this warning?**

_____

_____

Jesus used a warning to alert His disciples to the dangers of false teachers.

3. *Promise.* You can apply the promises of the Bible to your life unless a specific promise applies to someone else or is limited to another time. If the promise comes with conditions, you must follow those conditions to reap the promise.

✝ **Read Matthew 7:7. What is the condition that must be met to benefit from this promise?**

_____

When Jesus said, " 'Ask, and it shall be given to you,' " He meant that you must endure and persist in the practice of prayer before you can have assurance that God will hear your prayer. In contrast to this verse, God's promise in Acts 27:22-24 that no man on the ship with Paul would die applied personally to Paul. If you are in danger, you might hope and pray for the same kind of protection, but you cannot claim this verse as a universal promise.

4. *Command.* Both a command and a warning are spoken with a sense of obligation and order to the reader. The difference between these two is that the warning sounds an alarm, and the command is a specific call to action.

✝ **Read Matthew 28:19. Is this a command or a warning?**
❑ **Command** ❑ **Warning**

Jesus was calling all of His followers to action, so this is a command. He was not merely sending out a signal of danger. Peter similarly gave a command when he wrote, "Like the Holy One who called you, be holy yourselves also in all your behavior" (1 Peter 1:15).

Connectives are another area of biblical grammar you will find helpful to understand. Suppose someone says to you, "I didn't come to your party because I was sick." The last three words of the sentence explain why he didn't come to the party. The word *because* is a connective introducing those three words, *I was sick.* Connectives are words that link together the parts of sentences. Each part of the example is called a clause because each part has a subject and a verb. The connectives join the clauses of the sentence. There are many types of connectives, and each type can give different information about what the biblical writer is saying.

Connectives in the Bible

Time: *after, before, when, while*
Cause: *because, since, for*
Effect: *then, so, thus*
Purpose: *that, so that, in order that*

Some connectives show time. At least four connectives are in this group.

✝ Read the following passages and identify the connective in each. Note the chronological relationship of events that each connective establishes.

Matthew 26:32: _____

Acts 19:1: _____

1 Timothy 1:12-13: _____

Acts 2:37: _____

When a biblical writer uses one of the connectives *after, before, when,* or *while,* he places the events of one of the clauses either before, after, or at the same time as the events of another clause. Sometimes it is important in reading and understanding the Bible just to know the time relations between various clauses. Observing the time connectives can help you understand this.

Some connectives show the reasons behind certain actions. At least three connectives are in this group.

✝ Read the following passages and identify the connectives. Note the relationship between cause and effect.

1 John 2:12: _____

2 Corinthians 13:2-3: _____

2 Corinthians 4:18–5:4: _____

The connectives *because, since,* and *for* show the relationship between cause and effect, with the emphasis on the cause. When you see these connectives, the writer is probably saying, "*Because of the reason I am stating,* this result is taking place."

Another group of connectives reverses the emphasis to introduce or show results. At least three connectives are in this group.

✝ Examine the following passages and identify the connective in each. Again, carefully note the relationship between cause and effect.

2 Thessalonians 2:14-15: _____

Galatians 6:2: _____

1 Corinthians 14:24-25: _____

The connectives *then, so,* and *thus* also show relationship between cause and effect but with the emphasis on effect. When a writer uses one of these connectives, he is probably saying, "Because of the reason I am stating, *this result is taking place.*"

The final group of connectives shows purpose. At least two connectives are in this group.

✝ Read the following passages and identify the connective in each.

1 John 5:13: _____

Hebrews 13:6: _____

The connectives *that, so that,* or *in order that* emphasize the purpose or reason for an action to be taken.

As you read and study the Scriptures, note the time relationships, the relationship between cause and effect, and the reasons or purposes that are indicated by the way connectives are used. Often, the clue you receive from the connective used makes the difference in the way you understand and interpret a passage.

Understanding the relationships among the different **parts of speech** is another area of grammar that will enhance the effectiveness and skill with which you can use the other kinds of Bible study you have practiced during this study.

Verbs show action or existence. Verbs have tense, meaning that they show time relationships. Verbs can speak of something that is happening now, has already happened in the past, or will happen in the future. These tenses are called present, past, and future. Observing the tense of a statement is important in understanding and applying what it means.

✝ Read the following verses. Then draw lines across the columns to match the references with the correct tenses that are used.

John 14:26	Past
1 Corinthians 11:18	Present
Ephesians 2:1	Future

In John 14:26 Jesus made a promise for our future relationship with God through Christ. As we live with Him in the days ahead, the Holy Spirit will teach us things about God that we need to know. In 1 Corinthians 11:18 Paul wrote about differences that were currently seething in the church at Corinth. In Ephesians 2:1 Paul wrote that his readers had been dead in their sins in the past, but now they were alive in Christ.

Verbs also have active and passive voice. The active voice shows the subject acting or carrying out the action. The passive voice shows the subject receiving the action.

✝ Identify the voice of the verbs in the following verses.

1 Corinthians 3:6	❑ Active	❑ Passive
Ephesians 2:8	❑ Active	❑ Passive

In 1 Corinthians 3:6 Paul used the active voice to indicate that God caused the spread of the gospel in Corinth. In Ephesians 2:8 Paul used the passive voice to emphasize that we do not save ourselves, but we receive God's mercy.

A **noun** is the name of a person, place, or thing. A proper noun is the name of a particular person, place, or thing. The names of people are proper nouns, and in the Bible these names often describe the individual's spiritual potential. The name Jesus means *savior*, and the name Peter means *rock*. Some proper nouns used as names of places also describe something about the significance of the location. The term Decapolis in Mark 7:31 means *10 cities*. It is a reference to 10 Greek cities across the Jordan River where pagan influence was felt in New Testament days. In Acts 1:19 the name Hakeldama means *field of blood* and refers to the field in which Judas Iscariot took his life. You can often find the meaning of a proper name by using a concordance.

Pronouns are words used in place of nouns. The word for which the pronoun stands is called its antecedent. In Acts 8:4 Luke described a group of people by saying, "Those who had been scattered went about preaching the word."

† Find in Acts 8:1 the antecedent of the pronoun *those* in verse 4. Write the antecedent here.

The antecedent of *those* refers not to the apostles but to ordinary Christians driven from Jerusalem by the persecutions of Jews. Ordinary Christians were spreading the gospel.

Adjectives modify nouns and pronouns. **Adverbs** modify verbs, adjectives, and other adverbs. Their presence adds vitality and descriptive details to a sentence. In 1 Peter 1:4 Peter used adjectives to describe our Christian inheritance as "imperishable and undefiled and will not fade away." These vivid words describe a reward that cannot be taken away with the passage of time, the appearance of decay, or the presence of failure. In Titus 2:12 Paul used adverbs to urge us to live "sensibly, righteously and godly." These words picture someone who has self-restraint and complete commitment to God.

This week you completed a study of three keys to understanding the Bible: word study, biblical images, and the grammar of the Bible. We hope you were not bored by these detailed studies but were excited to see the way God inspired the biblical writers even in the most minute details to infuse His Word with significance and profound spiritual meaning. Next week you will study the last two keys for understanding the Bible.

✝ Test your knowledge of this week's Scripture-memory verse by writing it here from memory.

_____

_____

_____

_____

How is God sanctifying you as you walk with Him?

_____

_____

Review the previous weeks' Scripture-memory verses.

✝ Close this week's study in prayer praising God for His transforming Word.

Week 9

Keys to Understanding the Bible: Topics and Doctrines

Day 1
How to Study Topics in the Bible

Day 2
Practicing a Topical Bible Study

Day 3
Types of Doctrinal Bible Study

Day 4
Discovering One Book's Teaching About Doctrine

Day 5
How to Study a Doctrinal Passage

Scripture-Memory Verse
We urge you, brethren, admonish the unruly, encourage the fainthearted, help the weak, be patient with all men.
1 Thessalonians 5:14

T oday you will begin the second of a two-week study of keys to understanding the Bible. You studied three keys last week and will examine two more this week.

You have already learned about word study, biblical images, and the grammar of the Bible. This week you will learn how to study the topics and doctrines of the Bible. All of these keys have in common a narrow focus on specific elements of the Bible that will increase your Bible-study skills and deepen your understanding of the Bible's message.

Day 1
How to Study Topics in the Bible

Topical Bible study is the study of the topical teachings in the Bible. You may limit the topic to a single book, such as a study of the teaching in the Book of James about the use of the tongue. You may also trace the topic throughout Scripture, such as a study of the miracles in the Bible. The topic can be narrow, such as prophecies about Jesus' birth, or it can be broad and lengthy, such as prophecies in the Bible. A topical study can include topics that are important for churches, such as the roles of and requirements for church leaders. Husbands and wives can study the biblical topics of parenting and husband-wife relationships. Business people can study what the Bible says about handling money. Teachers can study Jesus' principles of teaching.

Topical Bible study can involve the study of a doctrine, such as the nature of God or the work of the Holy Spirit. It can also involve a practical matter like the ministries of a local church. The purpose of topical study is not just to satisfy curiosity. The focus must be on ways you can apply the topic to your life.

Topical Bible study is important because it provides a logical and orderly method of studying the Bible. The Bible's instructions and guidelines appear throughout Scriptures. You can use the topical method of study to bring together in an orderly manner all the Bible teaches about the use of time, money, or another suitable subject. Also, the use of topical Bible study can provide a balanced understanding of biblical teaching. For example, Galatians 6:2 says, "Bear one another's burdens, and thereby fulfill the law of Christ." In contrast, Galatians 6:5 warns, "Each one will bear his own load." A study of a topic like encouraging other Christians can help you discover which burdens you should bear and which burdens require help.

Topical Bible study also provides variety in individual study of the Scriptures. There is no limit to the variety of topics available for individual study. It is a type of study that fits well with the study of a book of the Bible. After you have studied a book like 1 Peter, you can study it again to examine such topics as God's directions for meeting suffering, the Christian and government, church leaders' duties, and Christ's example. This study will enrich what you have already learned from your investigation of the message in the entire book. In this way, topical Bible study helps you apply the Bible to daily living.

Some reference Bibles have already done much of the work necessary for topical study. Some contain many varieties of topical studies listed in the back of the Bible. These references contain verses of Scripture in which you can continue to investigate the topic. You will need only to look up the references. Other study Bibles include an encyclopedia that is helpful.

The method of topical study you will learn teaches you to use a concordance or a topical Bible to do your own study. The encouragement and excitement you will receive as you do your personal investigation can become an incentive to continue your Bible study.

✝ **Read the Book of James and identify topics you might want to study. Use the chart below to list each topic and record the chapter and verses that deal with that topic.**

Topic	Reference

Here is the process to follow in a topical Bible study.

1. *Select a topic for study.* The topic you select should be one in which you have a spiritual interest or need information.

2. *List related words.* This list should include synonyms, phrases, or ideas that have something in common with your topic. If you are studying the tongue, you might list such related terms as *words, speaking, boasting, cursing, blessing, utterance, instruction, reproof,* or *words of knowledge.*

3. *Find Bible references to your topic.* As you use a concordance and a topical Bible to find references, be careful to collect only verses that relate to your topic. Some New Testament references to the tongue refer to a spoken language rather than offering moral instruction about the tongue. Words like *blessing* and *boasting* show different ways of using the tongue. In looking at these words, however, be selective in choosing among the verses that describe the types of tongue usage. If your interest is the spiritual use of the tongue, add only verses that help you understand this topic.

4. *Write an observation or a question about each reference.* Be certain that your comments accurately reflect the context of the verses. Your comments might be a summary of the verse, the meanings of important words, insights about why the verse was written, and ways it applies to your life. Include questions about issues you don't understand.

5. *Write an outline.* Group Scripture references under appropriate subtopics. For example, in studying the tongue, you may find that some verses fall under categories like good uses of the tongue, bad uses of the tongue, controlling the tongue, or God's judgment of the tongue. As you review the verses you have gathered, a logical division will become clear to you. Include several subtopics under main topics. Each subtopic should contain a list of the references to the verses that support that subtopic. You will have an outline you can use in teaching or in sharing your ideas with others.

6. *Summarize your outline.* The outline provides an overview of what you have studied. A summary helps you condense what you have learned into a few words.

7. *Write applications.* List ways you can apply your topical study to your relationship with God, to your own life, to your relationships with others, and to the church.

As you study certain topics in the Bible, you may want to limit your research by restricting your study to one book. A study of the tongue can be a broad study. Both the Books of Proverbs and James have extensive teachings on the use of the tongue. Helpful insights about the use and abuse of the tongue can be found from a study of either book.

Tomorrow you will practice what you have learned about topical Bible study.

Doing a Topical Bible Study

1. Select a topic for study.
2. List related words.
3. Find Bible references to your topic.
4. Write an observation or a question about each reference.
5. Write an outline.
6. Summarize your outline.
7. Write applications.

✝ Your final Scripture-memory verse of this course is 1 Thessalonians 5:14. Begin memorizing it by using the Scripture-memory card at the center of your workbook.

Day 2
Practicing a Topical Bible Study

Yesterday you were introduced to topical Bible study, and you learned seven steps for completing this method. Today you will practice a topical Bible study. Then we will compare notes.

✝ Do a topical study of confrontation in the experiences of Jesus, Paul, and Peter. Gather Bible-study resources available to you and complete your study before reading further. Use the worksheet "Topical Bible Study" on page 190. (A master copy of this worksheet can be found on page 223.)

Topical Bible Study

Topic: _____

Related words: _____

_____

Bible references and observations: _____

_____

_____

_____

Outline   Summary

_____   _____

_____   _____

_____   _____

_____   _____

_____   _____

_____   _____

Ways to apply the study—
• to your relationship with God: _____

• to your own life: _____

• to your relationships with others: _____

• to the church: _____

Now let's debrief your work. The following process corresponds to the steps in topical Bible study that you considered yesterday.

1. *Select a topic for study.* Several years ago I listened with interest to a speaker who said that confrontation is an important ministry for any Christian. He defined *confrontation* as a word of encouragement or warning given by one Christian to another in need. His message sparked my interest.

2. *List related words.* I began my study by listing phrases, ideas, or synonyms that relate to the idea of confrontation. Among those were *exhort (exhortation), encourage, support,* and *rebuke.*

✝ **What other words or phrases did you list? Write them in the margin.**

3. *Find Bible references to your topic.* Looking up the key words in a concordance, I found these Bible references on the subject of confrontation: Acts 20:2; 1 Timothy 5:1,20; and 1 Thessalonians 5:14. I also selectively read through portions of the Bible in which spiritual leaders were confronting their followers and urging them to action. I quickly realized that so much material was available that it would be better to limit it to the New Testament. Knowing that so much material in the Bible is related to confrontation is the reason I began by limiting your assignment to confrontation in the experiences of Jesus, Paul, and Peter. For this limited area alone I found passages dealing with confrontation from the life of Jesus, the ministry of Paul, and the leadership of Peter. Some of those are Matthew 4:19; 13:45-58; 18:15-17; Mark 2:1-12; 8:33; 11:15-18; 14:35-36; Luke 16:14-15; Acts 1:15-26; 2:14-40; 5:1-11; 7:51-52; 9:4-6,15-16; Romans 16:17; 1 Corinthians 5:3-5,13; Galatians 1:6-10; and Titus 3:10-11. Some of these passages depict persons confronting other persons. Others show God and persons talking about needs and problems.

✝ **How does this group of references compare with the ones you listed on your worksheet? Circle the ones I listed that you did not list. You may want to add these to your list.**

4. *Write an observation or a question about each reference.* Next I asked the following questions about the references I listed.
- Who is doing the confronting?
- Who is being confronted?
- Why is the confrontation necessary?
- What method of confrontation is used?
- What are the results of the confrontation?

As I used these questions in my study, I was able to get a better understanding of a number of facts. For example, in Matthew 18:15-17 Jesus gave instructions for confronting a brother who has sinned or strayed. The method used is direct personal encounter. In Galatians 1:6-10 Paul confronts an entire church. This confrontation was necessary because church members were being misled by false teaching. Use these examples to evaluate the kinds of observations you made as you studied.

5. *Write an outline.* Here is how I began my outline.

I. Jesus and the ministry of confrontation
   A. Jesus confronted hypocrisy (see Luke 16:14-15).
   B. Jesus challenged others to action (see Matthew 4:19).
   C. Jesus challenged others to gain greater understanding (see Mark 8:33).

✝ Complete the outline for Paul and Peter.

II. Paul _____

_____

_____

_____

_____

_____

_____

III. Peter _____

_____

_____

_____

_____

_____

6. *Summarize your outline.* The last two steps are more personal than the preceding steps because they reflect needs. Maybe your summary statement was something like this: The church must practice the ministry of confrontation to prevent believers from slipping into sin (see Matthew 18:15-17; 1 Corinthians 5:3-5,13).

7. *Write applications.* Your summary should have provided material you used to apply your topical study to your life.

We hope you found topical Bible study to be a practical and engaging way to assemble Bible teachings on a subject that interests you. When you give focused attention to the Bible's teachings on a subject, it is easier to understand God's direction for this area of your life and to apply it as He has instructed.

Day 3
Types of Doctrinal Bible Study

Today you will begin learning the final key to understanding the Bible. Doctrinal Bible study is an effort to learn what the Bible teaches or assumes about the foundational beliefs of the Christian faith—topics like God, Christ, the Holy Spirit, humanity, salvation, and the church.

Begin your look at doctrinal Bible study by testing what you already know.

✝ Write T or F to indicate whether you think each of the following statements is true or false.

___ 1. Truths of the Bible are easy to understand because they are presented in a systematic, organized manner.

___ 2. Some biblical truths can be discovered by carefully reading the Bible.

___ 3. Examination of Scripture reveals that the biblical writers carefully avoided making assumptions.

___ 4. Surprisingly, no blocks of Scripture are purely theological in content.

As you study this session, you will discover how you should have responded.

To learn from doctrinal Bible study, you must fit together what the Bible teaches about the various doctrines because the Bible's treatment of the topics is not organized systematically. (Number 1 is false.) Its teachings about God, Christ, and other doctrines don't appear in a logical order. Doctrinal Bible study allows you to bring together through careful reading what the Bible says in its statements about various aspects of God's truth. (Number 2 is true.) Without doctrinal Bible study, the doctrines of the Bible may appear disconnected. A study of the doctrines in the Bible gives you an organized understanding of biblical beliefs and makes it easier for you to teach your beliefs to others.

At least three types of doctrinal study can be done. One is to study the many teachings and beliefs about God that are not formally stated but are assumed by the Bible writers. For example, the writers assumed the existence of God. They did not argue for it, seek to prove it, or labor about the issue. They assumed it as fact. (Number 3 is false.)

You can discover other assumptions when you read books in the Bible. Let's look at several examples.

✝ What assumption did Paul make in 1 Thessalonians 1:4?

_____

_____

Paul said that he knew God's choice of the Thessalonians. Paul therefore assumed his readers were God's elect, God's children.

✝ What assumption is made in 1 Thessalonians 5:2?

_____

_____

Paul mentioned that it is common knowledge that "the day of the Lord will come just like a thief in the night." He assumed that Jesus' return would be unexpected and without announcement.

In 1 Corinthians 15:1-23 Paul assumed that Jesus' resurrection is evidence that Christians have life after death. Paul plainly stated this in verses 20-23. It is a logical conclusion from his words.

Sometimes a Bible writer spoke to his readers with the words *we know*. Paul did this in 2 Corinthians 5:1, and his use of *we know* shows a belief or an assumption he makes. You can learn some of a writer's assumptions by looking for statements like this. In his Letter to the Philippians, Paul made a number of assumptions you can discover by carefully reading the book.

✝ Read Philippians 1—2 and list three doctrinal assumptions Paul made.

1. _____

2. _____

3. _____

Here are assumptions we noticed. You may have identified different ones. Paul accepted the certainty of Christ's second coming (see 1:6,10). Paul knew that God hears our prayers (see 1:3-4). Paul had confidence that God would complete His work of salvation in believers (see 1:6; 2:12-13). Paul assumed the existence and work of the Trinity (see 1:19; 2:6,11). Paul was certain of Christ's identity as the preexistent son of God who came to earth, died on a cross, and was exalted as Lord of the universe (see 2:6-11).

A second type of doctrinal study you can do is to collect information on subjects or topics that are prominent in a given book or text. The Book of Ephesians deals in detail with the doctrine of the church. The Book of Hebrews teaches the humanity of Christ. This type of doctrinal study closely resembles topical study and follows many of its principles. It differs from topical study only in that it is a study of a doctrine or a theological statement.

A third type of doctrinal study gives detailed treatment to sections of a book that are largely doctrinal in their content. (Number 4 is false.) James 2:14-26 addresses the relationship between faith and works. Romans 3:21-31 teaches justification by faith. You can turn to Hebrews 11 to understand the true nature of faith in God. The topic of Christ's resurrection is fully treated in 1 Corinthians 15. You can learn the content of these passages by using analytical Bible study to examine doctrinal sections.

Over the next two days you will learn more about the second and third types of doctrinal Bible study, and you will have opportunities to practice what you learn.

✝ **By now you should have learned this week's Scripture-memory verse. Write it here from memory.**

_____

_____

_____

_____

Types of Doctrinal Bible Study

1. Study the doctrinal assumptions made by a biblical writer.
2. Discover one book's teaching about a doctrine.
3. Examine a doctrinal passage.

Day 4
Discovering One Book's Teaching About a Doctrine

Yesterday you learned that there are three types of doctrinal studies.

✝ Check the doctrinal study you practiced yesterday.
❏ Discover one book's teaching about a doctrine.
❏ Study the doctrinal assumptions made by a biblical writer.
❏ Examine a doctrinal passage.

> ## Completing a Doctrinal Bible Study
>
> 1. Discover the doctrine being treated.
> 2. Identify passages that treat the doctrine.
> 3. Study each passage and record your observations.
> 4. Write an outline of the doctrinal passages.
> 5. Summarize your outline.
> 6. Record applications to your life.

Yesterday you learned how to perform a doctrinal study simply by discovering the writer's assumptions. Today you will learn how to study what one book says about a certain doctrine. Follow these steps to learn the doctrinal teaching of a single book of Scripture.

1. *Discover the doctrine being treated.* This is accomplished by carefully reading the book several times. Each reading will help you understand a teaching or an emphasis the book makes about God, Christ, salvation, the church, the Holy Spirit, or other doctrines. If you want to trace a subject of doctrine through a certain book, be sure to use a book that thoroughly treats the subject. You would not want to use the Book of James to study the Holy Spirit because that is not a major emphasis in James. However, James makes several references to the second coming of Christ and to events that

will happen when Jesus returns (see James 1:12; 4:12; 5:7,9). You can learn where to find full discussions of doctrinal topics by reading about those topics in a Bible dictionary or encyclopedia. There you will learn which books treat the subjects in some detail.

2. *Identify passages that treat the doctrine.* Sometimes you can locate in a concordance the word in which you are interested as it is found in that book of the Bible. Sometimes you cannot find the word; in that case, you must carefully read through a book to learn what it teaches about the doctrine.

3. *Study each passage and record your observations.* Practice the principles of analytical Bible study if you have difficulty interpreting any of the passages. You may also need to look for more information in a commentary or another Bible-study resource. However, do not do this until you have recorded insights from your personal study.

Today you will practice a doctrinal Bible study by exploring one book's teaching about a doctrine. Because doing this kind of study can require a great deal of time, we will help you take a few shortcuts.

✝ **Duplicate and use the worksheet "Doctrinal Bible Study" on page 199 to practice the first three steps you have studied so far. Your assignment is to discover what the Book of Hebrews says about the humanity of Christ. Normally, you would read the Book of Hebrews several times, identifying the passages that deal with Christ's humanity and comprehending the context of each passage. We will speed the process by telling you that the relevant passages are 2:17-18; 4:14-16; 5:1-10; and 7:23-26. List the relevant passages on the worksheet. Study each passage and record your observations. Complete these steps before continuing.**

Doctrinal Bible Study

Doctrine: _____

Bible references and observations: _____

_____

_____

_____

_____

Outline   Summary

_____   _____

_____   _____

_____   _____

_____   _____

_____   _____

_____   _____

Ways to apply the study—
• to your relationship with God: _____

• to your own life: _____

• to your relationships with others: _____

• to the church: _____

4. *Write an outline of the doctrinal passages.* Group scriptural teachings under appropriate subtopics, as you learned to do with topical Bible study.
5. *Summarize your outline.* Your summary should condense your study into a few words.
6. *Record applications to your life.* Apply your doctrinal study to the four areas you have considered throughout this course: your relationship with God, your own life, your relationships with others, and the church.

☩ Complete the remaining steps on your copy of the "Doctrinal Bible Study" worksheet before you continue.

The insights you gained from your doctrinal study should have equipped you to complete the following statements. Although some may seem to be similar, each clarifies a different aspect of Christ's humanity.

Hebrews 4:15: Christ can sympathize with the weakness of human beings because …

_____

Hebrews 2:17: Christ's participation in the human condition allows Him to …

_____

_____

Hebrews 2:18; 4:15-16: Because of Christ's demonstration of obedience, He is able to …

_____

_____

Hebrews 2:18; 4:15-16: Because Christ did not sin in the midst of His temptation, He is able to offer believers ...

_____

Hebrews 5:8: Christ learned the meaning of obedience by ...

_____

Hebrews 7:25: Because Christ lives to intercede for us ...

_____

_____

_____

Compare your outline with the one that follows. Perhaps you can improve this outline by adding ideas from your outline. And perhaps you can use some ideas from this outline to improve yours.

The Helpfulness of Christ's Humanity
I. His sufferings taught Him the full meaning of obedience (see 5:8-10).
   A. They secured for Him a maturity in His obedience.
   B. They gave Him every qualification for His priesthood.
   C. They obtained a glory from the Father in His exaltation.
II. His experiences provide encouragement for believers (see 2:17-18; 4:15-16).
   A. They show an example of victory.
   B. They allow mercy and grace for the tempted.
III. His atonement prevents separation from God for believers (see 2:17).
IV. His intercession secures complete salvation for believers (see 7:25).

Your observations and outline don't have to be identical to ours. The important thing is that they focus on the central ideas you have learned from your study and that they form a strong foundation for application.

Day 5
How to Study a Doctrinal Passage

You are learning three ways to do doctrinal Bible study.

✝ Name two types of doctrinal study you have learned.

1. _____

2. _____

You have already learned and practiced studying the doctrinal assumptions made by a biblical writer. You have also learned to discover one book's teaching about a doctrine. Today you will learn how to study a Bible passage that treats a special doctrine or teaches an important emphasis. This type of doctrinal Bible study is actually a special type of analytical Bible study dealing with a passage that is chiefly doctrinal.

Let's use this type of study to understand the doctrine James is teaching in James 2:14-26. Our first step is to perform a careful analytical study of the passage. Recall the principles of analytical Bible study you learned in week 4.

Principles of Analytical Bible Study

1. Write a paraphrase.
2. Use observations and questions.
3. Summarize the content.
4. Make a comparison.
5. Apply the passage.

✝ Read James 2:14-26. Follow the above principles to analyze this passage. Review week 4 if you need to. Record your work on the chart "Analytical Study of James 2:14-26" on page 203. Complete your study before reading further.

Analytical Bible Study of James 2:14-26

Paraphrase	Observations and Questions	Summary	Comparison	Application

Now let's process your work. You could paraphrase the verses only after careful reading and meditation. Check your paraphrase against a contemporary translation to make sure you did not depart from the writer's meaning.

We included these observations and questions.

- Notice that the *New American Standard Bible* translates James 2:14 as "Can that faith save him?" How does this differ from merely saying, "Can faith save him?"
- What is the meaning of the word *justified* in James 2:21,24?
- To what kind of problem is James addressing?
- Study the Old Testament passages in which Abraham is mentioned (see Genesis 15:6; 22:1-19). Notice that the incident of Genesis 15:6 mentioned in James 2:23 occurred before the incident of Genesis 22:1-19 mentioned in James 2:21. According to James, what did the incident in Genesis 22:1-19 prove about the incident in Genesis 15:6?
- In what sense was Rahab justified by her deeds? Find information about her in Joshua 2.

You also should have summarized in a sentence or two what you learned about James 2:14-26, what you believe the biblical writer meant, and how the passage may be used.

Compare the relationship of this teaching to such passages as Romans 3:21-31; Galatians 2:17-21; and Ephesians 2:8-10. Notice the close similarity in wording between the Romans passage and the passage here. Paul says that we are "justified by faith," while James says that we are "justified by works."

†Is there a difference in the meaning of the word *justify* as used by Paul and James? Explain what you discovered in your study.

_____

_____

_____

You probably needed to consult a commentary or a Bible dictionary for this one. Although Paul's and James's teachings seem to contradict each other, this is not the case. It is a matter of emphasis. Paul emphasized that justification comes by faith, as opposed to human works, which cannot earn God's acceptance. James explained that true faith is not limited to merely a confessing faith, like that of the demons, but must extend to a committed faith that expresses itself in good works. In other passages Paul also taught that faith results in a transformed life characterized by good works (see Romans 12; 2 Corinthians 5:17; Ephesians 2:10).

The application of the James passage no doubt demanded careful thought. Notice that James 2:14-20 shows the nature of a dead faith. This kind of faith can't meet human needs and can't show an inquirer that it is genuine. In James 2:21-26 we see that genuine faith results in an obedient life. This kind of faith led Abraham to show his obedience to God by offering Isaac and also led Rahab to offer protection to the Jewish spies. You should have recorded modern applications of these words to your life.

This brings you to the end of your two-week study of keys to understanding the Bible.

† **List the five keys to understanding the Bible you have been studying the past two weeks.**

1. _____

2. _____

3. _____

4. _____

5. _____

Using the tools of word study, biblical images, the grammar of the Bible, topical Bible study, and doctrinal Bible study can help you focus on specific words and topics in the Bible. Your Bible study can be expanded and enriched as you apply these tools.

✝ Write this week's Scripture-memory verse from memory.

_____

_____

_____

_____

Have you applied this verse this week? Describe how you have used or will commit to use it soon for Kingdom purposes.

_____

_____

✝ Review all the Scripture-memory verses.

In Closing

You have reached the end of this study. We pray you have gained valuable skills and insights that will enhance your reading, understanding, and application of the Bible. We also pray that this experience will increase your lifelong love for and devotion to learning and living God's Word, your authoritative and trustworthy guide for life's journey. Your life will be transformed by the One whose truths are revealed on its pages.

✝ Close your study in prayer. Commit to God to spend time in His Word and seek a deeper relationship with Him so that your life will be transformed into the likeness of Jesus.

❧❧ Leader Guide ❧❧

Don Atkinson

Welcome to leading a group study of *God's Transforming Word: How to Study Your Bible*. This guide provides practical suggestions for making this an exciting study. Begin preparing for the sessions by examining the following information.

• Remember that attending group sessions is not a substitute for individual study. The group study is based on the assumption that each member has completed the daily work at home.

• The group session plan will cover the previous week's individual study. The only exception is the introductory session.

• It is vital to the success of the study that you gather resources like concordances, Bible dictionaries, Bible atlases, and Bible commentaries to use in the sessions. Provide multiple copies when possible. These resources can be found in your church media library, at a public library, or from your pastor's or other staff ministers' library.

• Familiarize yourself with the leader plan for each session and with the content of *God's Transforming Word*. Faithfully work through the week's daily lessons to experience the process members will follow.

• As a service to participants, make multiple copies of the charts and worksheets that appear throughout the material. Masters are clearly identified with several located on pages 219-223. Tell members that these forms can be duplicated for use in Bible study after this course has ended.

• Several sessions call for resource persons. Enlist these persons well in advance. Let them know exactly when you will expect them and how much time they will have. Be certain that they have the materials they need.

• Each session asks you to review the week's Scripture-memory verse with members. Vary the way you do this each week. Ideas include calling for group recitation from the same translation, asking volunteers to recite for the group, instructing individuals to write the verse on paper, and having partners recite the verse to each other. Always provide an opportunity for members to check their work.

• Emphasize commitment to the study and the covenant with the group. This study will require time and effort.

• As the group leader, adopt a sense of mission about this study. Some members will begin a lifetime of Bible study as a result of this experience. Some members will use Bible-study tools for the first time. Be sensitive to those who become discouraged. Make yourself available to help them throughout the study. Your attention and encouragement can keep them involved.

• Enlist participants prior to the introductory session. The most promising sources are adult Sunday School departments and classes, adult discipleship groups, and men's and women's Bible-study groups. Announce that this study can help participants develop Bible-study skills. Explain that this study will require the commitment to do daily work as well as participation in weekly group sessions.

• Provide a meeting room with tables and chairs. Gather materials such as a chalkboard, newsprint or poster board, colored markers, and masking tape.

With this information in mind, you are ready to prepare to facilitate group sessions.

Introductory Session

Session Goals

After this session members will be able to—
- state why they wish to be part of the study;
- identify Bible-study tools they will need to use during the study;
- commit to and follow the requirements for Scripture memorization, daily individual study, and group participation;
- identify four aspects of hunger for God's Word and explain why each aspect is vital in studying the Bible.

Preparing to Lead the Session

1. Order a copy of *God's Transforming Word: How to Study Your Bible* for each member.
2. Carefully study the introduction (p. 6).
3. Cover part of a wall in the room with newsprint or poster board.
4. Prepare a poster listing the steps for successful Scripture memorization (pp. 12-13). List only the first statement under each step. Be prepared to briefly summarize each step.
5. Gather the following Bible-study tools and display them on a table in the room: several translations of the Bible, study Bibles, topical Bibles, commentaries, Bible dictionaries, Bible encyclopedias, concordances, and Bible atlases. These can be borrowed from the church media library. Get multiple copies if possible. Reserve these resources for the entire study. Make arrangements for members to check them out.
6. Enlist someone who is a good Bible student to give a five-minute testimony on the topic "How Bible Study Satisfies My Spiritual Needs."
7. Prepare for each member a covenant sheet with the following statement.

Group Covenant

I commit myself to do the daily work necessary to complete *God's Transforming Word*, to memorize the weekly Scripture verses, and to meet with the study group weekly for mutual encouragement and instruction.

Signed _____

Date _____

8. Prepare sheets with the following questions:
- What brought us to this study?
- What personal goals do we hope to attain?
- How can we assist each other?
- What weekly contact can we make to encourage each other?

Leading the Session

1. As participants arrive, instruct them to go to the newsprint or poster board and write their names along with a word or symbol that depicts their need to learn how to study the Bible. Take a few minutes to let members introduce themselves and to explain what they wrote or drew.
2. Distribute copies of *God's Transforming Word*.
3. State the goal of this course: to help members develop skills for reading, understanding, and applying God's Word. Give a brief overview of the course, using "What You Will Learn" (pp. 6-7).
4. Explain how the course works and the value of completing each day's material. Explain how the weekly group sessions provide opportunities to review, answer questions, and share experiences from their previous week's work.
5. State that members will memorize one Scripture passage each week. Demonstrate how the Scripture-memory cards are to be removed from the center of the workbook and used. Display the

poster and summarize the steps for successful Scripture memorization. Point out the discussion of each step on pages 12-13 for future reference.

6. Call attention to the display of Bible-study tools. Explain how participants can check out these resources. Encourage them to begin building their libraries. Strongly recommend they buy or borrow at least a Bible dictionary, commentary, and concordance for this study. Point them to the helpful resources on page 14.

7. Divide members into four small groups. Assign one aspect of spiritual hunger to each group: dependence on the Holy Spirit, eagerness to learn about God, a teachable attitude, and discipline. Refer the groups to the appropriate sections on pages 7-11. Ask the small groups to discover why their topics are vital to Bible study. Allow 15 minutes for groups to prepare and 2 to 3 minutes each for reports.

8. Ask the person enlisted to testify on how Bible study satisfies spiritual needs.

9. Distribute copies of the covenant sheet. Ask members to sign it if they want to participate.

10. Divide into pairs the members who have agreed to participate. Explain that these partners will serve as encouragers for each other. Distribute the assignment sheets and ask the partners to discuss the questions for 5 minutes.

11. Remind members to complete week 1 before the next session. Close in prayer for the study and for members' increased spiritual hunger.

Session 1
Guidelines for Interpreting the Bible

Session Goals
After this session members will be able to demonstrate an understanding of the guidelines for interpreting the Bible by—

• explaining the meaning of each guideline;
• using Scripture passages to illustrate these guidelines.

Preparing to Lead the Session
1. Complete the daily lessons in week 1.
2. Prepare a poster "Guidelines for Interpreting the Bible" and list the following guidelines:
   • Understand the writer's meaning.
   • Observe the context.
   • Accept the limits of revelation.
   • Identify the type of writing.
   • Use the Bible to interpret itself.
Use masking tape and paper to cover each entry.
3. Prepare listening sheets "Guidelines for Interpreting the Bible" and the guidelines listed in step 2. Leave writing space between each one.
4. Have available several Bible commentaries.
5. Prepare the five assignment cards that follow.

The Literal Meaning
1. Read Isaiah 55:12-13 and 1 Corinthians 16:1-4.
2. What do you think the writers literally meant? Does one passage seem more literal than the other?
3. Are there words or phrases in either passage that cannot be taken literally?

The Context
1. Read Matthew 6:3.
2. Could someone misuse this verse to prove that a person should not make a stewardship pledge or allow the church to keep a record of giving?
3. Read Matthew 6:1-4. What does verse 3 mean in its context?

The Limits of Revelation

1. Read 2 Timothy 3:14-17.
2. What does this passage teach about the specific purpose of Scripture?
3. Identify areas of human knowledge that the Bible does not deal with.

The Type of Writing

Locate a passage in the Bible that fits each of the following categories: narrative, parable, poetry, prophecy, and letter.

The Bible as Interpreter

1. Read John 6:52-58. In this passage Jesus spoke of believers eating His flesh and drinking His blood. Some people have found this passage puzzling. How would reading the entire chapter help in understanding what Jesus meant by eating His flesh and drinking His blood?
2. Read Exodus 16. How could this passage help a person understand John 6?
3. Read Mark 14:22-24. This text describes the meaning of the Lord's Supper. How could this passage help a person understand John 6:52-58?

Leading the Session

1. Welcome members and open with prayer.
2. Review the memory verse: Ephesians 4:32.
3. Allow members to share experiences or difficulties from the past week's study. If you sense that someone is having difficulty completing homework, contact that person this week.

4. Distribute the listening sheets and instruct members to write explanations of the guidelines as you present them. Take 10 minutes to review the five guidelines. Use the poster you prepared. Reveal each guideline as you discuss it.

5. Divide members into five small groups. If the total group is small, use five pairs; if necessary, use five individuals. Give each group one of the assignment cards. Tell groups to discuss their assignments. Invite them to use commentaries when appropriate. Make yourself available as needed. Allow 15 minutes for group work. Then have each small group report on its assignment.

6. Remind members of the covenants they signed. Encourage partners to stay in touch.

7. Remind members to complete week 2 before the next session. Close with prayer.

Session 2
Principles for Applying the Bible

Session Goals

After this session members will be able to demonstrate an understanding of the principles for applying the Bible by—
- writing a brief definition of each principle;
- classifying selected Bible promises as universal, limited, personal, or conditional.

Preparing to Lead the Session

1. Complete the daily lessons in week 2.
2. Enlist the pastor or another knowledgeable Bible student to give a 15-minute lecture on the five principles for applying the Bible in week 2.
3. Prepare listening sheets "Principles for Applying the Bible" and include the following:
- Apply the Bible according to its real meaning.
- Use the Bible as a Book of principles.

• Use the promises properly.
• Use a cross-cultural understanding.
• Use the Bible wisely.

Leave writing space between each principle.

4. Secure four pouch-type file folders. On the outside of each folder, print one of the following headings with a marker: *Universal, Limited, Personal, Conditional*. Attach the folders to a bulletin board with thumbtacks or to a wall with masking tape so that the folder pouch is open.

5. Prepare slips of paper with one of the following promise references written on them:

John 1:12	John 16:24
John 5:24	Philippians 4:7
Isaiah 26:3	John 14:13-14
Proverbs 3:5-6	John 15:7
Matthew 6:14	Jeremiah 29:13
Proverbs 3:9-10	2 Corinthians 12:9
Philippians 1:6	Psalm 28:7
Proverbs 22:6	Psalm 46:1
James 5:16	Philippians 4:13
Acts 1:8	Philippians 4:19
John 16:13	James 4:6

Leading the Session

1. Welcome members and open with prayer.
2. Say the Scripture-memory verse, 1 Peter 5:7.
3. Introduce the pastor or the other person you enlisted to give the 15-minute lecture on principles for applying the Bible. Distribute the listening sheets. Instruct members to listen and write a definition of each of the five principles.
4. Give out the Bible references and ask each person to look up the verse or verses. When everyone has had time to read the verses silently, have the verses read aloud. Explain that they are all promises found in the Bible. Ask each person to place the reference in the file folder that represents the type of promise it is. Allow the group to agree or disagree with the way each person

classified each promise. If there is disagreement, let the group discuss where the promise belongs.

6. Remind members to complete week 3 before the next session. Close with prayer.

Session 3
Ways to Do Bible Study: Synthetic Bible Study

Session Goals

After this session members will be able to demonstrate an understanding of synthetic Bible study by—

• participating in a discussion of synthetic Bible study;
• using the book-summary chart.

Preparing to Lead the Session

1. Complete the daily lessons in week 3. Make sure you understand how to use the paragraph-summary form and the book-summary chart.
2. Provide several Bible translations.
3. Draw the paragraph-summary form and the book-summary chart on sheets of newsprint or poster board, or use overhead cels.

Leading the Session

1. Welcome members and open with prayer.
2. Review this week's verse, Philippians 3:10.
3. Discuss any questions, problems, or difficulties members encountered in this week's study.
4. Review the meaning of synthetic Bible study. Explain that it is a type of study that looks at a book of the Bible as a whole. As you define it, let members ask questions and make comments.
5. From your personal work in day 2, demonstrate the use of a paragraph-summary form on the newsprint, poster board, or overhead cel.
6. From your written responses in day 3, demonstrate the use of a book-summary chart on

the newsprint, poster board, or overhead cel. Make certain everyone understands how to use these charts.

7. Divide into three small groups and give each group a large sheet of newsprint or poster board and markers. Explain that the groups will use book-summary charts for the next activity. Assign each group one of the Bible books studied in week 3: Philemon, Philippians, or 1 Peter. Ask groups to discuss their week's study of the book and report on the first chapter or major division. Instruct groups to report the title or theme, and conclude their reports by giving a summary of the key ideas in the first chapter or major division. As groups report, ask members to check their work in week 3 against the groups' charts.

8. Remind members to complete week 4 before the next session. Close with prayer.

Session 4
Ways to Do Bible Study: Analytical Bible Study

Session Goals
After this session members will be able to demonstrate an understanding of analytical Bible study by—
- identifying the five elements of analytical Bible study and placing them on the analytical Bible-study chart;
- writing either a paraphrase or a summary of a Bible passage.

Preparing to Lead the Session
1. Complete the daily lessons in week 4.
2. Provide several modern Bible translations.
3. Copy the analytical Bible-study arch (p. 75) on a large poster. Leave blank the five sections of the arch. Provide marking pens.

4. Enlist five members to give three-minute explanations of the following elements of analytical Bible study.
- Write a paraphrase.
- Use observations and questions.
- Summarize the content.
- Make a comparison.
- Apply the passage.

5. Prepare assignment sheets for everyone and include the following:
- Write a paraphrase of Colossians 1:15-18 without using a Bible translation. After the paraphrase is written, compare your paraphrase with a modern translation.
- Write a summary of the content of Colossians 1:15-18, using contemporary Bible translations to help you.

6. Provide paper and pencils.

Leading the Session
1. Welcome members and open with prayer.
2. Review this week's verses, Philippians 4:6-7.
3. Give participants an opportunity to share experiences related to the past week of study.
4. Call on those enlisted to make the brief presentations. As each person presents, have someone use a marker to fill in the appropriate section of the arch on the poster you made. Make certain that all members understand each point.
5. Distribute the assignment sheets. Ask each member to choose and complete one of the two activities. Provide paper and pencils.
6. After the paraphrases and summaries are written, divide both the paraphrasers and the summarizers into pairs. Give the pairs five minutes to share their work with each other.
7. Remind members to contact their partners each week for mutual help and encouragement.
8. Remind members to complete week 5 before the next session. Close with prayer.

Session 5
Ways to Do Bible Study: Background Bible Study

Session Goals

After this session members will be able to demonstrate an understanding of background Bible study by—

- stating reasons background Bible study is important;
- practicing using Bible-study tools that provide background information.

Preparing to Lead the Session

1. Complete the daily lessons in week 5.

2. Prepare a five-minute lecture on the importance of background Bible study.

3. Gather the following aids for this session: concordances, reference Bibles, Bible dictionaries, Bible atlases, and Bible commentaries.

4. Set up four tables or learning centers in the room. If possible, use adjoining or nearby rooms for two of the learning centers.

5. Make signs to designate the learning centers: *1. Using a Concordance; 2. Using a Bible Dictionary; 3. Using a Bible Atlas; 4. Using a Bible Commentary.*

6. Enlist four capable Bible students to lead five- to eight-minute studies on the use of the following Bible-study tools: 1. How to use a Bible concordance; 2. How to use a Bible dictionary: 3. How to use a Bible atlas; and 4. How to use a Bible commentary. Contact these leaders well in advance of the session and ask them to give instructions and a practical demonstration of how the assigned Bible-study tool can be used in background Bible study. Explain that each of them will make the presentation four times. Provide newsprint, markers, paper, pencils, and other supplies these persons need.

Leading the Session

1. Welcome members and open with prayer.

2. Say the Scripture-memory verse, John 4:14.

3. Give a five-minute lecture on the importance of background Bible study. Invite them to write the reasons this is important as you share them.

4. Announce that this session will focus on using Bible-study tools for background Bible study. Point out the four learning centers that have been set up to help them review the use of these tools. Explain how each person will visit each learning center during this session.

5. Divide members into four small groups. Number the groups 1 through 4. Group 1 begins at the learning center where a concordance will be studied. Group 2 goes to the table focusing on using a Bible dictionary. Group 3 goes to the table where a Bible atlas will be studied. Group 4 goes to the table focusing on a Bible commentary.

6. After eight minutes, give a signal to instruct the groups to rotate to the next table. Continue until each group has visited the four tables.

7. Reassemble the group for closing comments. If time permits, ask members to share their experiences with background Bible study.

8. Remind members to complete week 6 before the next session. Close with prayer.

Session 6
How to Apply Bible Study: Biographical Bible Study

Session Goals

After this session members will be able to demonstrate an understanding of four areas to apply Bible study by—

- sharing with another person the ways they applied John 13:34-35;
- completing a biographical study.

Preparing to Lead the Session

1. Complete the daily lessons in week 6.

2. Prepare a poster or overhead cel "Four Areas to Apply Bible Study" followed by the four areas:

- To your relationship with God
- To your own life
- To your relationships with others
- To the church

Be prepared to review the four areas based on the material in day 1.

3. Prepare for all members copies of the worksheet "Biographical Bible Study" (p. 122) and of the chart "How I Can Apply a Biographical Study" (p. 127). Have available pencils and paper.

4. Gather Bible concordances, dictionaries, encyclopedias, and commentaries on Acts.

Leading the Session

1. Welcome members and open with prayer.

2. Review this week's verses, John 13:34-35.

3. Answer questions about this week's work. If a member is having problems with the study or is becoming discouraged, plan a personal contact.

4. Present a brief review of the four areas to apply Bible study, using the poster or cel.

5. Divide the group into pairs. Ask members to share with their partners ways they applied John 13:34-35 in the activity on page 116.

6. Reassemble the group. Distribute the worksheets and charts. Ask each person to use these to do a biographical study of Philip, the evangelist. Explain that the account of Philip is found in the Book of Acts. Point out the concordances, commentaries, encyclopedias, and dictionaries available in the room. Ask members to work on their own and share the resources.

7. If time permits, allow volunteers to share their findings and applications with the group.

8. Remind members to complete week 7 before the next session. Close with prayer.

Session 7

How to Apply Bible Study: Character-Trait and Devotional Bible Study

Session Goals

After this session members will be able to demonstrate an understanding of character-trait Bible study and devotional Bible study by—

- listing the eight steps for doing a character-trait Bible study;
- doing a character-trait Bible study with a partner;
- participating in a devotional Bible study with the group.

Preparing to Lead the Session

1. Complete the daily lessons in week 7.

2. Provide paper and pencils for members.

3. Prepare copies of the worksheet "Character-Trait Bible Study" (pp. 219-20).

4. Use a large sheet of newsprint or poster board to make a replica of the worksheet "Devotional Bible Study" (p. 145). Prepare another poster "Ways This Passage Can Be Applied" and include the following areas:

- To your relationship with God
- To your own life
- To your relationships with others
- To the church

Use two sheets of newsprint, if necessary, to allow room to record responses.

5. Collect concordances, topical Bibles, and Bible dictionaries for use in this session.

Leading the Session

1. Welcome members and open with prayer.

2. Review this week's verses, James 1:2-4.

3. Distribute blank sheets of paper and pencils. Ask members to list steps for doing a character-trait Bible study (pp. 132-33) without referring to

the workbook. Review the steps and ask members to fill in those they were unable to list.

4. Ask members to work with their encouragement partners to do a 15-minute character-trait Bible study. Assign the character trait of loyalty. Distribute copies of the worksheet "Character-Trait Bible Study." Ask members to record their findings on the worksheet. Each pair will need a topical Bible, a concordance, or a Bible dictionary.

5. Reassemble the group. Allow 10 minutes for reports. Call for a general sharing time rather than have each group report.

6. Lead the group in a devotional Bible study of 1 Corinthians 12.
  • Ask each member to read the passage and think about it for a moment.
  • Use the outline of the poster "Devotional Bible Study" to lead the group through the study. Ask for group participation. Then lead the group to work together to complete the poster "Ways This Passage Can Be Applied."

7. Ask for brief comments about members' contacts with their encouragement partners. Urge partners to plan a time to talk each week.

8. Remind members to complete week 8 before the next session. Draw attention to the worksheet "Word Study" (p. 164). Ask members to be prepared to share their word studies in the next session. Close with prayer.

Session 8

Keys to Understanding the Bible: Word Study, Images, and Grammar

Session Goals

After this session members will be able to demonstrate an understanding of word study, biblical images, and grammar of the Bible by—

  • listing the six steps for doing a word study;
  • sharing with the group their word-study notes from the past week;
  • locating various figures of speech in selected Bible passages;
  • identifying Bible statements as facts, warnings, promises, or commands;
  • identifying the connectives used in selected Bible passages.

Preparing to Lead the Session

1. Complete the daily lessons in week 8.

2. Use six sheets of newsprint or poster board and markers to make six posters with the steps for doing a word study, using the first sentence of each numbered point (see pp. 159–62). Conceal these posters until you are ready to use them. If you use newsprint, fold up the bottom of the poster and attach it to the top with pieces of masking tape. When you are ready to use the posters, reveal them one at a time.

3. Prepare a five-minute summary of the six steps for doing a word study.

4. Use newsprint or poster board to reproduce the worksheet "Word Study" (p. 164).

5. Prepare group-assignment cards with the following information.

Metaphor

Psalm 44:3; Isaiah 59:1; Luke 8:21; Luke 12:32; Luke 22:31; John 10:16

Simile

Isaiah 1:8; Jeremiah 23:29; Matthew 23:37; Matthew 24:27; Luke 10:3; 1 Thessalonians 5:2

> ## Synecdoche
> Judges 12:7; Joel 3:10; Micah 4:3

> ## Hyberbole
> Deuteronomy 1:28; John 21:25; Romans 4:19

> ## Euphemism
> Leviticus 18:6; Acts 1:24-25

> ## Metonymy
> Genesis 42:38; Luke 16:29; Romans 3:27-30

> ## Personification
> Psalm 114:1-8; Matthew 6:34

> ## Rhetorical Question
> Romans 4:9-10; Romans 8:31-35

6. Make four placards with the words Statement of Fact, Warning, Promise, and Command.

7. Be prepared to summarize the functions of connectives used in the Bible.

8. Provide pencils, paper, and several King James Versions of the Bible.

Leading the Session

1. Welcome members and open with prayer.
2. Say this week's verse, 1 Thessalonians 5:23.

3. Present a five-minute review of the six steps for doing a word study. Display each poster as you explain it. Cover the poster when you are finished with the explanation.

4. Distribute paper and pencils. Ask members to list the six steps for doing a word study. When everyone is finished, uncover the posters for members to check their answers.

5. Guide members to share with the group their word-study notes from the past week's work. Use the poster "Word Study" to guide a time of general sharing.

6. State the importance of understanding figures of speech in Bible study. Ask members to form pairs. Give each pair an assignment card and a *King James Version* of the Bible. If you have more pairs than cards, make duplicate assignments. If you have fewer pairs than cards, choose assignments from the cards. Instruct each pair to review the definition of its assigned figure of speech from day 3 or 4, read the assigned passages from the King James Version, and find its assigned figure of speech in the passages. Call for pairs to define their figures of speech and to give one example from their Scripture.

7. Shift the focus to the grammar of the Bible by emphasizing the meaning a knowledge of grammar can add to Bible study. Ask eight members to come to the front of the room. Ask four members to bring their Bibles and space themselves across the front. Give the other four members the placards with the words *Statement of Fact, Warning, Promise,* and *Command.* Ask the members with Bibles to read the following verses one at a time. After each is read, the member with the placard that correctly identifies the grammatical form of the verse should move and stand beside the person who read. Ask members if they agree that the verse has been correctly identified. Then continue with the other three

passages. Answers are provided in parentheses.
- Matthew 6:33 (command)
- Matthew 6:1 (warning)
- Matthew 6:24 (statement of fact)
- Matthew 6:30 (promise)

8. Briefly summarize the functions of connectives that are commonly used in the Bible. Test the group's understanding by reading the following Scriptures, emphasizing the italicized words, and ask volunteers to complete the statements to indicate the function of the connective word used. Answers are provided in parentheses.
- When John said, "We love, *because* He first loved us," he was stressing (cause).
- When Jesus said, "I came *that* they might have life," He was stressing (purpose).
- When Paul said, "*While* we were yet sinners, Christ died for us," he was stressing (time).
- When Paul said, "So then, brethren, stand firm and hold to the traditions which you were taught," he was stressing (effect).

9. State that the next session will be the final one. Remind members to complete week 9 before the next session. Close with prayer.

Session 9
Keys to Understanding the Bible:
Topics and Doctrines

Session Goals

After this session members will be able to demonstrate an understanding of topical and doctrinal Bible study by—
- completing a topical Bible study;
- identifying three types of doctrinal Bible study;
- discussing the study they did this week.

Preparing to Lead the Session

1. Complete the daily lessons in week 9.

2. Make a poster from the worksheet "Topical Bible Study" (p. 190). Leave adequate room for writing responses as you use the poster during the session.

3. Be prepared to summarize the steps for completing a topical Bible study.

4. Prepare three placards listing the three types of doctrinal Bible study:
- Study the doctrinal assumptions made by a biblical writer.
- Discover one book's teaching about a doctrine.
- Examine a doctrinal passage.

Do not display the placards in advance.

5. Be prepared to name an example of each type of doctrinal study if members are unable to do so.

6. Make copies of the bookmark "Next Steps for Bible Study."

Leading the Session

1. Welcome members and open with prayer.

2. Say this week's verse, 1 Thessalonians 5:14.

3. Display the poster "Topical Bible Study." Review each step.

4. Ask members to turn to the topical Bible study they completed on page 190. Ask a different volunteer to name the way he or she completed each portion of the worksheet as you record the response on the poster. Discuss as needed.

5. Ask whether members can recall the three types of doctrinal study identified in day 3. As each type is named, attach the appropriate placard to the wall.

6. After all three placards are displayed, ask members to think of examples of the three types of doctrinal studies that could be done. Give examples if members have difficulty.

7. Ask members to team with their encouragement partners. Ask partners to compare and discuss the ways they completed the worksheet "Doctrinal Bible Study" (p. 199). Allow no more than 15 minutes for discussion.

8. When partners have completed their discussions, ask if members have questions about how to do doctrinal Bible study.

9. Emphasize the importance of continuing to practice the Bible-study skills they have learned in this course. Distribute the bookmarks and review the ideas for the next steps members can take. Point out the copies of Bible-study charts and worksheets in the appendix (pp. 219-23), which members can duplicate for future use.

10. Ask encouragement partners to end the study by praying for each other's continued spiritual growth through the regular study and application of God's Word.

Next Steps for Bible Study

1. Choose longer books like Genesis or 1 Corinthians for synthetic Bible study.

2. Use the principles of analytical Bible study to study brief Bible passages. If you are a Bible-study teacher, prepare your lessons by using the principles of analytical Bible study.

3. Use background Bible study to learn about a passage's historical, geographical, cultural, or sociological background.

4. Complete biographical studies of Bible characters like Caleb and Joshua in the Old Testament or Barnabas and Mary Magdalene in the New Testament.

5. Do character-trait studies of various Bible figures to learn qualities that God wants to see in His children.

6. Regularly use devotional Bible study to apply passages to your life.

7. Examine the words, images, and grammar of a passage to deepen your understanding.

8. Use the principles of topical Bible study to examine Bible topics that interest you. Use the methods of doctrinal Bible study to study the doctrines of salvation, the Holy Spirit, or spiritual gifts. Or study an entire book to discover its doctrinal teachings.

9. No matter what type of Bible study you choose next, be sure to apply the teachings to your life. Bible study is incomplete without this important step.

Character-Trait Bible Study

Trait: _____

Dictionary definition: _____

_____

Synonyms: _____

Antonyms: _____

Bible definition and teachings: _____

_____

Summary of Bible teachings: _____

_____

Reflections:

• What are some benefits of this trait in my life and in the lives of others?

_____

_____

• What are some problems this trait could produce in my life or in the lives of others?

_____

_____

•MASTER COPY • DUPLICATE BEFORE USING•

219

• Is there a promise or warning from God about this trait? If so, what is it?

_____

• What factors produce this trait? _____

_____

• What effect does this trait produce in the life of the church?

_____

_____

• Is this trait a part of God's character? ❏ Yes ❏ No

Ways to apply the study—

• to my relationship with God: _____

_____

• to my own life: _____

_____

• to my relationships with others: _____

_____

• to the church: _____

_____

Devotional Bible Study

Scripture reference: _____

Summary of the passage's meaning/teaching:

_____

_____

_____

_____

_____

_____

Is the teaching timeless or temporary? ❑ Timeless   ❑ Temporary

Related Scripture references and their teachings:

_____

_____

_____

_____

_____

_____

Applying Devotional Bible Study

Scripture reference: _____

1. Pray that God will give you insight about the application of the passage.

2. Meditate on the passage, asking yourself:

Is there any—
❑ **P**romise to claim or praise to offer God?
❑ **E**xample to follow or avoid?
❑ **A**ction or attitude to change?
❑ **C**ommand to obey?
❑ **E**rror to avoid?

3. Ways this passage can be applied—

• to your relationship with God: _____

_____

• to your own life: _____

_____

• to your relationships with others: _____

_____

• to the church: _____

_____

4. Memorize the verse(s).

5. Ways you can put the application into practice: _____

_____

• M A S T E R C O P Y • D U P L I C A T E B E F O R E U S I N G •

Topical Bible Study

Topic: _____

Related words: _____

_____

Bible references and observations: _____

_____

_____

_____

Outline   Summary

_____   _____

_____   _____

_____   _____

_____   _____

_____   _____

_____   _____

Ways to apply the study—
• to your relationship with God: _____

• to your own life: _____

• to your relationships with others: _____

• to the church: _____

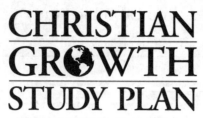

CHRISTIAN GROWTH STUDY PLAN

Preparing Christians to Serve

In the **Christian Growth Study Plan (formerly Church Study Course)**, this book *God's Transforming Word: How to Study Your Bible* is a resource for course credit in the subject area Personal Life of the Christian Growth category of diploma plans. To receive credit, read the book, complete the learning activities, show your work to your pastor, a staff member or church leader, then complete the following information. This page may be duplicated. Send the completed page to:

Christian Growth Study Plan
127 Ninth Avenue, North, MSN 117
Nashville, TN 37234-0117
FAX: (615)251-5067

For information about the Christian Growth Study Plan, refer to the current Christian Growth Study Plan Catalog. Your church office may have a copy. If not, request a free copy from the Christian Growth Study Plan office (615/251-2525).

God's Transforming Word: How to Study Your Bible
COURSE NUMBER: CG-0102

PARTICIPANT INFORMATION

Social Security Number (USA ONLY)	Personal CGSP Number*	Date of Birth (MONTH, DAY, YEAR)
Name (First, Middle, Last)	Home Phone	
Address (Street, Route, or P.O. Box)	City, State, or Province	Zip/Postal Code

CHURCH INFORMATION

Church Name		
Address (Street, Route, or P.O. Box)	City, State, or Province	Zip/Postal Code

CHANGE REQUEST ONLY

☐ Former Name		
☐ Former Address	City, State, or Province	Zip/Postal Code
☐ Former Church		Zip/Postal Code